FORCES THAT
FORM YOUR FUTURE

KEVIN GERALD

Tulsa, Oklahoma

TABLE OF CONTENTS

PREFACE

Whatever Will Be...

Most people share a common curiosity about the future. The curiosity is demonstrated by the flourishing business of 1-900-Psychic numbers appearing on our television screens. People want to know:

- "What is going to happen in my life tomorrow, next week and next year?"
- "Who am I going to marry?"
- "What is going to happen in my career?"
- "Am I going to be successful?"
- "Is my marriage going to last?"

Horoscopes, fortunetellers and palm readers are literally "cashing in" on this powerful curiosity.

Unfortunately most people assume that the future is a complete mystery that they have little or no control over. Men and women often view themselves as "victims" of fate. These same people await their future circumstances totally dependent upon getting "a good break" or "lucky" in the events of life. Anyone who succeeds is seen as being at the "right place at the right time." Those who get comfortable with repeated and continual hardship take on a powerless motto of "whatever will be will be." If these people happen to be

Christians, their motto only changes *slightly*. They declare whatever happens is the will of God and the will of God is whatever happens. It's that same "whatever will be" concept dressed up in spiritual clothes.

Whatever Will Be Is Influenced by Me

This book is written as a challenge to the "whatever will be will be" approach to life. The will of God is not whatever happens. All you have to do is look around you and you can see that there are many things happening in the world today that are definitely not God's will. For example, poverty and violence is not God's will. God does not want to make our decisions for us. He insists on us governing our lives and deciding our futures. When going through a crisis many people ask "why is God doing this to me?" In reality, God didn't do it, they did. For example, a middle-aged man may wonder "why am I in this same low-paying job? Men much younger than me are making more money and having fun doing it and I'm stuck with this job I hate and can barely survive on!" A closer look, however, will reveal that the younger man probably chose to go to college, took time to choose a desirable career, invested in himself, disciplined himself, set goals and achieved them. The first man, on the other hand, left his future to the elements of time and chance.

Another common scenario among Christians and Christian leaders is to conclude that their problems are most often "an attack of the enemy." It is very common for believers to overlook the "natural" causes for their problems and rush to the conclusion of a spiritual attack. The fact is, however, that there is only one Devil and he is not omnipresent. Even when you add to that the 33 percent of angels that we refer to as "fallen angels," who are now involved in the mission of stealing, killing and destroying, it remains highly unlikely that most people experience strategic satanic attacks. The more appropriate explanation for repeated crises and constant problems lies in poor choices. The choices that determine our approach to life will inevitably influence our futures. Choices are God's gift of empowerment in our lives. Good choices maximize life's possibilities and poor choices maximize life's problems. Even God's involvement in our life is subject to our choices. With this in mind, you are now ready to explore the *forces that form your future.* Also keep in mind that these forces do not work individually but collectively to usher in our future. Similar to a recipe with various ingredients or an artist with various colors, the combining of these forces will produce a "flavor" or a "picture" called our future.

INTRODUCTION

"The secret things belong to the Lord our God, but the things revealed belong to us and to our children forever..."
— *Deuteronomy 29:29*

In this book, I won't attempt to explain the things that happen in our lives that we have no control over. Secret things are those exceptional circumstances that are unplanned, unexpected, unavoidable and inevitable. Our comfort, as a child of God, comes from knowing that secret things are subject to God's plan for our lives. What He permits is based on His knowledge of the future and how it can work in His plan for us. Contrary to what many may think, God doesn't get up early every morning and decide what the weather will be like in various places of the world. The weather is the result of a "system" God put into existence. He doesn't order droughts, floods, heat, blizzards as a type of entertainment for Himself. He "allows", *not* "orders" the weather. Occasionally, when He has someone praying for specific weather, He will interrupt the system on their behalf (James 5:17-18).

On a more normal basis, however, God allows the machinery of the universe to be His delegated authority, functioning as He created it to function; which means that in some circumstances, there will be thunder, storms and even lightening bolts. These are not a sign of God having a bad day and taking it out on us with those loud noises and special effects. In fact, He's not directly initiating the lights and sounds in the sky. It's just happening as part of the weather system. Some of what goes on in our lives is the same way. *It's just happening.* Not because God is mad at us or punishing us. In fact, He probably had nothing to do with the lightening bolt that hit your world. Our first response to the lightening bolt is usually, *"Why God?"* **That question...that moment that renders no explanation is the time of secret things in our lives.** Even though God didn't initiate it, He did allow it. We feel helpless and vulnerable. The lightening bolt hit our world and left us with a broken heart, a confused mind and a question of *"why?"* There is no explanation for secret things.

"...but the things revealed belong to us and to our children forever..."
— *Deuteronomy 29:29*

This book is about the revealed things; the wisdom and knowledge available to us today to form and shape our lives, our future and our destiny. If you can find it and understand it, it's a "revealed" thing. If it's taught in Scripture, can be found in the bookstore or learned from someone else's experience, it's a revealed thing. Our lives are mostly formed by revealed things.

My goal in writing this book is accomplished if a reader is awakened to the God-given opportunity of a lifetime; to help you, the reader, know that your life is a gift from God and what you do with it is your gift back to God. There are "forces" *within you* that are forming your future. This is why God works *within* us—because that's where the forces are that are shaping the quality and nature of our lives. *"For it is God who works in you to will and to act according to his will"* (Philippians 2:13).

God's plan, according to Jeremiah 29:11, is a great plan for your life. A plan to "prosper you and not to harm you . . . to give you a hope and a future." With that in mind, I want to encourage you to **see yourself as** *"partnering"* **with God to bring forth His great plan for your life and future.** Your future is not all up to God and it's not all up to you. See it as a partnership opportunity between you and God to hit the target of His will.

CHAPTER ONE

THE FORCE OF A SEED SOWN

"Whatever a man sows, he reaps..."

—*Galatians 6:7*

Envision your life and your future as an empty field...a piece of raw dirt given to you to do whatever you want to do with it. What would happen if you said to the field, "Give me some potatoes, give me some corn, give me..." Would the field respond? Would the dirt break open and deliver? Does a harvest come by wishing? Our individual futures are like the field. It doesn't respond to a wish, it only responds to a seed!

Now, let's take the scenario a bit further. What if we mistakenly put watermelon seeds in our field and then after realizing what we had done, said to the field, "I made a mistake, would you cancel those seeds and I'll go get the right ones?" Would the soil say, "No problem, I'll cancel that harvest"? Would the watermelon be denied? Can the field respond to a wish or only to a seed?

The law of the harvest insists that everything produces "after its own kind" (Genesis 1). Gorillas are subject to the law of the harvest. Two gorillas cannot produce a giraffe…horses cannot produce cows, etc. No matter what Darwin said, you are no monkey's uncle! The entire animal kingdom, all plants, all fruit-bearing trees and the seed of all living creatures are subject to the law of the harvest and can only produce "after their own kind." This spiritual law is not limited to plants and animals. It's equally potent in the more subtle areas of life. There is a harvest in: what we think about…what we say…what we do. . . .

Is It a Seed?

One of the most common questions Christians ask when someone suggests that they make a behavior or lifestyle change is, "Is it a sin?" To reap a desirable harvest in our lives, we must move beyond the question of, "Is it a sin?", to the question of, "Is it a seed?" The question is not just "Will it keep me out of heaven?", but also "What will it do to the quality of my life here on Earth?" (1 Corinthians 6:12) People who are harvest minded know that they have to move beyond being "sin conscious" and become "seed conscious." Christian people sow a bad harvest just like non-Christians. Christian wives sometimes sow seeds of negligence into their marriage... Christian parents sow seeds of anger into their children's future... ***The seed doesn't cancel because you are a Christian.*** It is subject to the law of the harvest and will produce "after its own kind." Our lives improve when we evaluate our thoughts, words and actions as "seeds" that will produce a harvest. I can't help but wonder if the people who voted prayer out of public schools have ever connected the harvest of lower SAT scores, increased classroom violence and overall loss of conscientiousness in schools with their decision to ban prayer. When we hand out condoms in school...when we legalize abortions...when we permit homosexuality to be presented as an alternative lifestyle... what do these "seeds" look like when they reach their maturity? Is it surprising that teenage pregnancy is so common? Is it surprising that we have a killer disease of AIDS on the loose? Is it a surprise that dysfunctional families are on every block? Is it a surprise that gang activity has increased?

TIME magazine published an article on the strange and violent behavior of "orphan elephants."

This phrase describes a herd of elephants in Africa that were separated from their parents and other mature elephants. The consequence now being discovered is an unharnessed aggression in the young males. Scientists have concluded that the lack of "mentorship" of these young males by older and more mature males has caused strange behavior. For example, rhinos living in the same area are being attacked and killed by these elephants. The wildlife conservationists are now transporting some of the older males back into the young herd of orphan elephants. They expect to see the older males now correct and mentor the younger elephants.

In America today we've witnessed the harvest of absentee fathers in our homes. Gang violence and other behavior problems in the youth of our nation are nothing more than a harvest resulting from lack of mentoring the next generation. None of this should surprise us if we recognize that they all began as a SEED.

Before a mistake can turn into a blessing, we have to do three things. First, we have to *take responsibility* for sowing the seed. Second, we have to *repent* and ask God to forgive us and third, we have to *redefine* the mistake as a blessing.

Sarah had been unable to have a child. So in a moment of discouragement and low self-esteem, Sarah suggested to her husband, Abraham, that he have children with their servant Hagar (Genesis 16). As soon as

Hagar is pregnant, tension fills the house. Sarah complains to Abraham...she blames Abraham...she mistreats and abuses Hagar. *Over the next few years Sarah complained about something that would have never happened had she not suggested it.* Now little Ishmael's presence was unavoidable. Everywhere that Sarah looked she saw Ishmael. Remember, once a word is spoken, once an action is taken, it is impossible to erase. "Ishmael" will be an undeniable part of your life. Sarah tries to get rid of him by sending him away. Some people think they can move, change jobs, get a new spouse, or go to a different church and their "Ishmael" will cease to exist. Unfortunately, the "seed" has brought forth a harvest. You can't change what has happened. There is only one way to treat the "Ishmaels" of our lives. Repent and let God turn your mistakes into blessings (Romans 8:28). I am convinced that if Sarah would have taken responsibility for her choices and repented of them, she could have sown seeds of unity into her family instead of the strife between Ishmael and Isaac that continues to this very day. The more we attempt to hide, cover or blame others for the "Ishmaels" in our lives the more miserable we become. When we take responsibility for poor choices, repent and stop complaining, God can turn those things that are despicable into something positive in our lives.

To Reap a Desirable Harvest,
Learn to Recognize a Harvest In a Seed

"Make a tree good and its fruit will be good, or make a tree bad and its fruit will be bad, for a tree is recognized by its fruit."

—Matthew 12:33

A tree is recognized by its fruit. We know an apple tree by the observation that apples are hanging on its branches. It doesn't take a rocket scientist to identify a banana tree, when bananas are all over it. It's quite simple to recognize a tree by its fruit. *On the other hand, if you are interested in producing a specific harvest, you must learn how to recognize a harvest in a seed.* Personally, I'm quite uneducated on the various kinds of organic seeds. If I walked into a seed store, I wouldn't know an apple seed from a sunflower seed. It's not important for me to recognize specific seeds because I'm not a farmer. I'm not trying to create a harvest of wheat or barley or oranges. But for the sower who wants a specific harvest in his fields, he must be able to recognize a harvest by looking at a seed. How terrible it would be for a farmer to think he's planting corn and find that he has actually planted strawberries. He doesn't want strawberries. He has purchased equipment to reap corn. He doesn't have a market for strawberries. Therefore, it is essential that he be able to look at a seed and see a harvest. It is too late to change the harvest after it has come forth. He must see it and select it while it is still a seed. In order to reap a desirable harvest, we must learn to recognize a harvest in...what we think about <u>before</u> we think it...what we say <u>before</u> we say it...what we do <u>before</u> we do it. Ask yourself before sowing a seed; will this seed produce a desirable harvest in my life? Will it...move me towards my goals or take me off track...move me closer or farther away from God...strengthen or weaken my marriage? Since there is a harvest in every seed, the ability to recognize the harvest <u>before</u> it's a harvest is the beginning step of creating a desirable future.

Seeds That Sow a Destiny

"The good man brings good things out of the good stored up in him..."
—*Matthew 12:35*

1. **The Seed of Desire** – The treasured ambitions and desires of our heart are seeds that can eventually be seen in our actions and heard in our words. What we want most takes precedence over what we want least. For example, some people want money more than they want their integrity. Therefore, in a moment of choice they compromise integrity to make a sale. Some ath-

letes want their college educations so they postpone their athletic careers. Some people want to please God more than their passion so they refuse premarital sex. The seeds of desire can be numerous. The wise sower will always seek the seed that represents the desired harvest of their life. By choosing the seed, the wise sower sets in motion a desired destiny. The "other" seeds of desire that produce an undesirable harvest will be constrained by the wise sower. The wise sower knows that seeds of desire (good or bad) will sow a destiny. He works at bringing forth "from the good stored up in him."

2. **The Seed of Satisfaction** – What we accept, allow and tolerate will exist. In a conversation with my grandfather, he informed me how he had grown up in an alcoholic environment. He told me how he made up his mind early in life to break out of that atmosphere and to make something of his life. He spent a lot of time at his grandparents' house as a young teenager avoiding the atmosphere at home. It was in that determined, unsatisfied state of mind that he attended a Lester Sumrall meeting and gave his life to God. While his siblings all struggled through life, he enjoyed a career with Exxon Oil Company, bought land, prospered and now both of his children, and all his grandchildren, are in full-time ministry. I'm not only proud of my grandfa-

ther, I'm thankful that he wasn't satisfied with the lifestyle he grew up in. He broke off an inherited influence that captured his siblings to enjoy a long, happy marriage, career and walk with God. *Man will never rise above his level of satisfaction.* Some people confuse satisfaction with contentment. Contentment has to do with peace in our spirit; something we can have regardless of our circumstances. Satisfaction on the other hand, would make no effort to improve circumstances. Keep this in mind: *Whatever* you accept, allow and tolerate *will exist.* When we begin to be dissatisfied, that is the "seed" of a better harvest.

3. The Seed of Discretion – *"Discretion will protect you, and understanding will guard you" (Proverbs 2:11).* Discretion is wisdom in choices. To be discreet means, "to be thoughtful or careful about what we say and do." People who are discreet realize that their words and actions will produce a harvest, so they consider what they are doing before they do it. In today's world the term "dysfunctional family" has become the trendy alibi for irresponsible behavior. Suddenly, all of our "no-brainer" actions are blamed on our upbringing in a "dysfunctional family." You may be thinking "I'm where I am because of my parents…they had alcohol addictions," or "they never expressed love." My point is that we all are still responsible for how we react to negative circumstances in our lives.

The seed of discretion can and has brought many people out of difficult and extremely negative surroundings into a life of hope and accomplishment. In my opinion, Ronald Reagan is one of the greatest presidents of all time and perhaps the greatest in this century. His biography reveals what most of us never knew about his family life. As a youth, Ronald Reagan often carried his drunken father from the yard or floor of their home and put him to bed. It is something we hear little about because he had chosen not to focus on that part of his life. He used discretion in what he thought and talked about. Some people just "blab" and then justify it by saying "Well, it's the truth!" Whether it is true or not, learning discretion with your words and actions can protect you from focusing on the wrong things. Discretion can help you avoid the trap of "victim mentality" that ruins thousands of lives today. Again, discretion is wisdom in choices. Remember, we often say "no" to one thing in order to say "yes" to another.

- You can't say yes to a welfare check every month and also say yes to a good job that will prosper you.

- You can't continue to receive "get well wishes" of sympathy when you are healthy.

- You can't park in the handicap parking and give up your handicap status.

- You can't still behave independently and be married.

- You can't increase without agreeing to decrease or invest something.

If you make choices that may not be easy to make, you are planting "seeds" called discretion that will help produce a desired destiny.

4. **The Seeds of Discipline** – "You can't have what you want to have, only doing what you want to do." Discipline is the self-mastery that causes a person to do things they may not enjoy doing in order to enjoy the benefits of having done them. If I had my preference, I would eat more burgers, pizzas, cakes and ice cream. Somebody says, "Oh, don't worry about it, eat without guilt...enjoy it...you only live once." That's exactly right. I do have one life and I have realized that I can't feel how I want to feel and also eat what I want to eat as often as I want to eat it! So, I have to do a couple of things I don't want to do...exercise and watch my eat-

ing habits! The seed of discipline is missing in the lives of many talented people. They remain governed by instant gratification doing what they want to do in the present and it causes them to never have what they really want in the future. Their full potential is never realized because they lack the seed of discipline.

Selective Seed Sowing

The reason it's important to identify seeds that sow a destiny is to improve your ability to apply something I call selective seed sowing. By selecting your seed, you create a predictable harvest. God created the universe to reap what is sown and produce only what is consistent with its own nature (Genesis 1:24). People who apply the principle of selective seed sowing trust the law of the harvest *("A man reaps what he sows." Galatians 6:7)* to return to them a harvest consistent with seed sown.

I'm never surprised when blessings find me. I get excited and thankful, but I've learned that I can expect blessings since I've lived my life to be a blessing. I expect people to give me good things because I'm a giver. I get upgrades on airline seating and upgraded hotel rooms just given to me. I have lots of friends who provide a consistent flow of encouragement. People go out of their way to help me and support me. Business owners consistently provide services and open doors on behalf of our ministry. None of this happens by coincidence. This same thing happens to anyone who is a sower of good seed.

A Seed Sown in Good Soil Produces a Harvest Exponentially Greater Than the Original Seed

A seed of corn grows into a stalk, which produces ears of corn, with each ear containing a bunch of kernels. This multiplication process begins with a single seed sown. By the same principle, if an eighteen-year old puts one dollar per day in a mutual fund, earning 15 percent, by the age of sixty-five, that one dollar per day will produce a return of $2.65 million. When considering the power of a seed sown, it's important to note that a seed can't produce a harvest until it's planted. Just having seed doesn't produce a harvest, sowing seed does!

Archeologists discovered seeds preserved in an Egyptian pyramid that were over two thousand years old. When scientists planted some of those seeds, they produced life. All that potential was "locked up" in the seed until the seed was sown. When a father doesn't express love to his children, it's like having seed in a barn. Unused talent is also like having seed in a barn. There is no harvest by holding seed. ***Don't hold your seed – sow your seed.***

Cast your bread upon the waters, for after many days you will find it again...whoever watches the wind will not plant; whoever looks at the clouds will not reap...sow your seed in the morning, at the evening let not your hands be idle, for you do not know which will succeed, whether this or that, or whether both will do equally well.

—Ecclesiastes 11:1, 4, 6

This chapter is an enthusiastic admonition to make seed sowing a daily part of our lives. A farmer has several options of what he can do with his harvest.

- He can hold (some of) his harvest.
- He can exchange his harvest (for money at market).
- He can consume (eat) his harvest.

None of these options, however, will produce another harvest. It's my understanding that when a harvest of corn comes in, the wise farmer always keeps the best ears of corn for "seed corn." He doesn't hold it, exchange it or consume it, but he replants it to produce another harvest.

People who take in without generously giving out will soon begin to see a shortage of good things coming their way. Holding what we have, consuming what we have, or exchanging what we have ("I'll do nice things if you pay me for it"), will not produce the harvest of unsolicited goodness and uncommon favor in our lives. Unsolicited goodness and uncommon favor comes to those who practice God's laws of daily generosity with an open hand and open heart approach to life.

What Is in Your House?

In 2 Kings 4, a distraught widow says to Elisha, "My husband is dead…we have debts and the creditor is coming to take away my sons to be slaves..." Elisha did not respond by assuming personal responsibility for this woman's plight. Instead, he asked her to carefully consider "What is in your house?" Her response was an indication that she underestimated the potential of what she had to produce what she needed. "Nothing," she replied, "except a little oil." It's easy to assume we have no seeds to sow when facing insufficiency and lack. However, it's important to remember that there will never be a day in our lives when we have nothing. We always have "something" and that "something" that looks like "nothing" is a seed that will produce the harvest we need in our lives.

The Schwab Center for investment research released a recent study that showed giving up potato chips with lunch could save $176.80 a year and generate $10,483.62 in twenty years, assuming a 10 percent return. Switching a double latté with whipped cream to regular coffee could save $429 per year, which becomes $27,028.07 at 10 percent return over twenty years.

When Moses complained to God that he was not talented and didn't have anything of usable worth to God, God asked him the question, "What is that in your hand?" (Exodus 4:2). God then instructed Moses to let it go – "throw it down." Everything you'll ever need in life begins as a seed in your house and hand. *The sowing of today's seed is the answer to tomorrow's need in your life.* For the distraught widow, the little oil became an endless supply of provision during famine; and for Moses, the familiar, common staff became an object of powerful influence greatly benefiting God's people.

I received an e-mail message of the following analogy, which is a great admonition for all of us to not overlook or underestimate the potential that God has put in our lives.

Whose Hands?

- A basketball in my hands is worth about $19.
  A basketball in Michael Jordan's hands is worth about $33 million.
  It depends whose hands it's in!

- A baseball in my hands is worth about $6.
  A baseball in Mark McGuire's hands is worth $19 million.
  It depends whose hands it's in.

- A tennis racket is useless in my hands.
  A tennis racket in Pete Sampras' hands is a Wimbledon Championship.
  It depends whose hands it's in.

- A rod in my hands will keep away a wild animal.
  A rod in Moses' hands will part the mighty sea.
  It depends whose hands it's in.

- A slingshot in my hands is a kid's toy.
  A slingshot in David's hand is a mighty weapon.
  It depends whose hands it's in.

- Two fish and five loaves of bread in my hands is a couple of fish sandwiches.
  Two fish and five loaves of bread in God's hands will feed thousands.
  It depends whose hands it's in!

Time Is What Happens
between Sowing and Reaping

If a person wants potatoes for dinner tonight, hopefully they didn't wait until this morning to plant them in their garden.

"Cast your bread upon the waters, for after many days you will find it again."

–Ecclesiastes 11:1

"At the proper time we will reap a harvest if we do not give up."
–Galatians 6:9

A friend of mine told me of a former missionary who was sick and could not get an accurate diagnosis on his illness. After continued tests and research, doctors identified the illness as a virus the missionary had contracted fourteen years earlier in the Philippines. The parasite had remained dormant in his body for fourteen years! Some harvests return sooner than others into the life of the sower. In fact, some seeds will produce harvest extending beyond our lifetime.

The Chinese bamboo tree appears to have no life the first four years after it is put in the ground. However, after four years of nurturing and watering the seed, it grows over ninety feet in the fifth year!

Your guarantee to an endless provision of unsolicited goodness and uncommon favor is in a daily habit of sowing good seed. When you are a blessing, you're sure to be blessed. When you give it will be given to you and the measure with which you sow, you will reap (Luke 6:38). The seeds we sow are a force forming our future.

CHAPTER TWO

THE FORCE OF A BELIEF

"According to your faith will it be done to you..."
—*Matthew 9:29*

Confronting Beliefs

To know what you will receive, confront your beliefs. We are usually apprehensive in discussing our beliefs until after they have been confirmed as accurate. However, when we believe something, even at a subconscious level, the power of belief will work to make what we believe a reality. In other words, it is interesting that our most compelling beliefs, whether positive or negative, typically become reality. Although it is undeniable that God's power is the source of human achievement, it is also undeniable that our favorite Bible stories would not have happened had it not been for a believer's mind-set. For example, what did Nehemiah believe about the restoration of Jerusalem? You don't have to read far into Nehemiah's story to conclude that he genuinely believed that Jerusalem could be restored. The city had been going downhill for 140 years. The streets were ghettos of hopelessness and poverty until one man's belief turned it all around. His faith led a restoration that took only fifty-two days to accomplish.

To investigate the mind-set of other Bible characters that experienced great victories, simply consider…

- What did David believe about his battle with Goliath?
- What did Abraham believe about Sarah's barren womb as she approached one hundred years of age?
- What was Peter believing when he stepped out of a boat and onto the water?

Now…

- What do you believe about your circumstances?
- What do you believe about your career?
- What do you believe about your children?
- What do you believe about your future?

By accurately discerning your own beliefs, you create an opportunity to change your beliefs. Why continue to believe something that can lead to undesirable circumstances? Why believe something that creates negative energy (worry and anxiety) in your life? Beliefs can be chosen and developed to create what is sometimes referred to as a "belief system". Once decided upon, your belief system will be a tremendous force in forming your future.

Five Questions to Help
You Confront Your Beliefs

1. Do I believe that God is a good God and that He wants to give me good things?

I remember a trip I took to Asia where my daughter had asked me to try to find her a specific kind of camera while I was there. I think I hit every camera shop in Hong Kong before finally finding the right one. Every time I was tempted to give up, I thought about the joy of being able to give her exactly what she wanted. That picture in my mind kept me going. I wanted so much to make her happy. In the same way, God wants to meet our needs, just as much as I wanted to put that camera in the hands of my daughter. How we see God and what we believe about His desire for us will affect how we approach Him. It is harder to approach someone for something when you don't think they will want to give you what you're asking for (Matthew 7:9-11).

2. Do I believe the Bible enough to make all of my decisions based on its guidance?

When you are dependent on a map, it helps if you believe in its accuracy. When we don't believe in the map, we defer to our own instincts. We've proven time and again, that human instincts can be severely inaccurate. Our belief in the Bible's accuracy will determine whether we act according to its guidance or not. A wavering belief leads to actions that are inconsistent with God's plan for life. An absolute belief, on the other hand, causes us to obey God and reject natural instinct. For example, a Christian person who is single may by instinct be attracted to a person who is not a Christian (attending church...living the Christian life). The Bible says we should not be in covenant relationship with unbelievers (2 Corinthians 6:14). That person must now make a decision that will reveal how much they believe the Bible's reasoning and guidance for their life.

3. What do I believe about my health?

In Luke 17:19, Jesus tells a leper "Your faith has made you well." Since then, medical science has confirmed the link between our faith and our physical health. Although some definitely enjoy a "miracle" or sudden healing from God, others are made well through a more gradual healing process. It is also true that negative beliefs such as worry and fear cause stress which then cause our bodies to break down physically. When this happens the condition is often compounded by specific negative beliefs about our physical condition.

In Bruce Larsen's book *There's a Lot More to Health Than Not Being Sick*, he states the following: In a recent survey, the American Medical Association asked several thousand general practitioners across the country, "What percentage of people that you see in a week have needs that you are qualified to treat with your medical skills?" Some replied 25 percent and some 1 percent but the average was 10 percent. In other words, by their estimate, 90 percent of the people who see a general practitioner in an average week have no medically treatable problem. Certainly they are ill and suffering real pain, but their problem is not chemical or physical and defies normal medical procedure. The survey went on to ask what the doctor did for these people. Most of the respondents said they prescribed tranquilizers such as valium. When asked what they would like to do for these people, most of the doctors said they would like to have had time to spend an hour a week talking to these patients about their lives, their families, and their jobs.

Even in our health it's undeniable that what we believe is affecting what we receive.

4. Do I believe that the things I hope for and pray for will be a reality in my life?

There is a difference in wishing and believing. When we believe something is impossible, our whole mind goes to work to prove "why" it's impossible. It is the duty of the mind to develop a rationale or reason to support our beliefs. Likewise, when we believe something is possible, our mind will go to work to show us "why" it's possible. When we are unsure, it is like having two attorneys in our mind, each arguing their case. Our most compelling belief will eventually declare victory and be established within our mind. This established thought is what the Bible refers to as a "stronghold." A stronghold can be good or evil, according to Scripture. A good stronghold is the well-developed, fortified place of faith. A bad stronghold, on the other hand, is a fortified place of negative and destructive thoughts in our minds. Strongholds are those beliefs we defend and fight for. When we establish our beliefs for those things we hope and pray for, we empower our prayers to become a reality.

5. Do I believe that everything that happens to me will benefit me?

If you don't, it won't! If you do, it will! When we believe there is something beneficial in every experience, we will look for and find the benefit. In the book of Genesis, we read the story of a man named Joseph. It seemed that no matter what happened to him, Joseph kept faith for his future. If he had been a man of doubt or resentment, his life would have been much different. Joseph's beliefs brought him repeated promotions. When he named his sons, his faith was obvious:

- *Manasseh:* "God has caused me to forget my troubles."
- *Ephraim:* "God made me fruitful in the land of my suffering."

When he reflected on his life of betrayal and the repeated injustices against him, he proclaimed, "What was intended for evil against me, God meant for my good"(Genesis 50:20).

Our Beliefs Affect Our Choices

On a recent family vacation in Hawaii, my family and I were just moving out into the water when I noticed a very concerned look on the face of a couple coming towards me. Here we were, happy and excited about going snorkeling and these people were obviously anxious to get out of the water. I could tell that the woman especially was anxious to say something to me. After our eyes met, I automatically said to her, "Is everything OK?" Her husband was reluctant but could not contain her as she blurted out, "There's a shark out there." What followed was a detailed description of a large shark in the vicinity we wanted to snorkel in. After telling ourselves that there was nothing to worry about and that sharks like that don't hurt people, we proceeded to go snorkeling. The next half hour was the worst! Every time I put my head down in the water, I would hear *"Jaws"* music. My head was messed up with scenes of a great white shark attack on the Gerald family. It wasn't long until those prevailing mind pictures led all of us to the beach. It is unlikely that we were in any real danger. On the other hand, the "shark" in my head would not be denied. The thought of a shark in the water influenced our choice to head for the beach. *The casual choices we make every day are influenced by invisible, yet persuasive, beliefs.*

Our Beliefs Affect Our Potential

For thousands of years, the flat world theory kept men from exploring the unknown world. Even the daring, bold explorers did not venture beyond certain points because of their belief that the world was flat and had an edge they could fall off of. How many beliefs have hindered progress in your life? Since beliefs influence our actions and dictate our behavior, it is only reasonable to see them as a force forming our future. However, many people still look at their own thoughts as having no real effect on the events and circumstances of their life.

In a booklet from the Successories Library, written by Dennis Wattley and Boyd Matheson, there is a story of a primary grade school teacher who, with the permission of the parents, told her class that recent scientific reports had verified that children with blue eyes had greater natural learning abilities than children with brown eyes. She had them make signs that they hung around their necks, designating them as blue or brown eyed. After a week or so the achievement level of the brown-eyed group fell measurably while the performance of the blue-eyed section improved significantly. Later she announced to the class that she had made a mistake. It was really supposed to be the blue-eyed individuals who were the weaker students and the brown-eyed ones who were stronger students. She told them that all babies were born with light blue eyes, then as they grew older and smarter their eyes turned darker to brown. Up went the image and achievement of the brown-eyed students and down tumbled the achievement of the blue-eyed children.

Be careful of the message you are communicating; it could pay dividends or it could have negative repercussions. Of course, you and I know, as that teacher did, that the performance of those students had nothing to do with the color of their eyes. It had everything to do with the beliefs in their heart. If a person believes that their troubled family history is something they can overcome, they will overcome. If you believe you are blessed and favored, you will be. If you believe your skin color doesn't change your potential, it won't. If you believe your potential is God-given and unstoppable, it will be!

Your Beliefs Affect Your Position of Power

In 1898, a construction party was building a railroad across Africa. Over a period of nine months, the railroad personnel were haunted by the presence of two man-eating lions. These lions were so cunning and crafty that they managed to get past barricades, huge fences, and around the clock armed guards to repeatedly drag screaming victims into the blackness of the night. These animals were tracked and hunted, but escaped time after time. Very strange things happened that caused the railroad workers to begin to think the lions were immortal. Guns failed to fire and heavily baited lion traps failed to work. One night, two men fired twenty shots at the distance of ten feet and did not hit the lion. The lions became known as "the Devil." If it had not been for one man, J.H. Peterson, refusing to believe the popular myth (that the lions were immortal), the railroad project would have been stopped. J.H.

Peterson finally succeeded in killing the man-eating lions, ending the nightmare.

This story is an example of how all of us act and react to life based on our beliefs. *When we believe a foe is undefeatable, it will be.* In fact, all my life I've heard Christians describe the Devil as having power to wreck and destroy them. These people sometimes lack the determination like J.H. Peterson. They fall into a belief that there's nothing they can do to make things better in their life. Their constant defeats are a result of their belief system, not the power of the Devil. The Devil is defeated, but until a person knows that he's powerless they will believe him to be powerful and unstoppable in their life. The bigger enemy then is not the Devil, but the Devil in their mind!

At our house we don't talk about the Devil, because we believe that the Devil has no power over our lives. That belief keeps me in my position of power and creates my reality. Other people's lives are destroyed by the "lion on the prowl" (1 Peter 5:8). Believing in who you are and what God has said about you is your protection against the myths of helplessness and defeat. These myths will circulate around you and most people will believe them. Their constant defeats will be the result of their belief system. Your never-ending victory lies in the same thing – a belief system.

Believing vs. Trying to Believe

"Everything is possible for him who believes" (Mark 9:23).

Jesus knew that God had created us with a power that was being overlooked by most people. He continually emphasized what the power of believing has on receiving. Jesus encouraged people to believe for what they desired and prayed for. He let us know that a person's beliefs can strengthen or sabotage their future. Recently, I read about some doctors in Texas that conducted a pilot study of orthoscopic knee surgery that used general anesthesia. Ten patients with sore, worn knees were assigned to one of three operations; scraping out the joint, washing out the joint, or doing nothing. In the "nothing" operation, doctors anesthetized the patient, made three cuts in the knee as if to insert the instruments and then pretended to operate. Two years after surgery, patients who underwent the "sham" surgery reported the same amount of relief from pain and swelling as those who had the "real" operations.

Studies like this have convinced even the most cynical critics to not overlook or deny the power of believing. Unfortunately, most people with flawed or self-sabotaging beliefs will need a major life experience to change the deep-rooted beliefs that are greatly influencing their daily life.

Believing is different than trying to believe. In the battle between a belief and what we try to believe, the authentic belief always wins. That is why in the above example, the doctor went beyond telling the patients that they had performed corrective surgery on their knees and actually "convinced" the patients that surgery had been done by giving them anesthesia and cutting on their knees. These patients were not "trying" to believe. In their minds the correction had been made on their knees and they fully expected to get better. Being convinced and fully persuaded is authentic, deep-level believing. In the first part of this chapter we asked ourselves five questions about our beliefs. As Christians, we sometimes are trying to believe what we know we should believe. Beliefs we don't want have stubbornly taken up residence within us and we need God's help, God's Word and a steady diet of supporting data to replace the deep-rooted doubts and fears with faith and authentic agreement with God.

CHAPTER THREE

THE FORCE OF RELATIONSHIPS

The Super Bowl is the most watched professional sports event in America. As the final seconds tick off the game clock, the camera goes from one happy player to another. Without exception, the winning players acknowledge, in the midst of their celebration, that they were there because they were part of a winning team. Across the field, another group of players are experiencing the pain of defeat.

This is a lot like life! The people we align ourselves with, can determine whether we win or lose in life. Relationships affect our lives and destiny. The Columbine School shooting was a tragedy etched on the walls of our memory. Cassie Bernel, with a gun to her head, would not deny her faith even though it meant the loss of her life. In the aftermath of the shooting, her parents would tell how Cassie had not always been a committed Christian. In fact, they told how she, herself, had once been a troubled teen participating in a party-lifestyle, writing letters of hatred and anger towards her parents and society. But a remarkable change had occurred in Cassie's life when she began hanging out with a different crowd. Her view of life had undergone a radical change to the point where people around her, including the gunmen, knew her as a committed Christian.

Cassie's story is a powerful example of how our relationships affect our lives and destiny.

"Stay away from a foolish man..."
—Proverbs 14:7

"He who walks with the wise grows wise but a companion of fools suffers harm."
—Proverbs 13:20

"Bad company corrupts good character."
—1 Corinthians 15:33

"Do not associate with anyone who calls himself a brother but is immoral...with such a man do not even eat."
—1 Corinthians 5:11

"As iron sharpens iron, so one man sharpens another."

—Proverbs 27:17

"Two are better than one…"

—Ecclesiastes 4:9

God-Assigned Connections Are in Your Life Right Now

God did not intend for anyone to succeed alone. Everyone is assigned to be "connected" to specific people. Those assignments are essential to the God-planned destiny for our lives. *Once you realize how vital your relationships are to your life and future, you will begin to see certain people as God-assigned connections.*

- David had a God-assigned connection with Jonathan.
- Joseph had a God-assigned connection with a butler.
- Esther had a God-assigned connection with a king.
- An Ethiopian crossing the desert had a God-assigned connection with Philip.
- Elijah had a God-assigned connection with Elisha.
- Twelve disciples had a God-assigned connection with each other.
- Ruth had a God-assigned connection with Naomi.

The purpose in the God-assigned connections is to perpetuate, nurture and complete God's plan for our lives. There are five areas where God is putting people in your life right now. Becoming aware of their presence is the first step to realizing God's purpose in putting them in your life.

Contacts – They network us.
Friends – They affirm us and are committed to us.
Partners – These people share a common interest or goal.
Mentors – They produce change in us.
Protégées – They learn from us.

God sends great people into all of our lives. How we treat them determines whether they can stay. The more you accurately identify the "role" of people God is bringing into your life, the greater the potential for your relationship there will be. My friend, Wellington Boone, wrote a book entitled, *Your Wife Is Not Your Momma*. (It's become my wife, Sheila's, favorite line whenever I ask for something!) When we get the roles right, we will experience the purpose for which God put them in our life. Failure to recognize roles can cause us to miss out on God's intention for us. For example, when you find a mentor, be content to be a student. Oftentimes, people who don't know how to treat a mentor that God has put in their life will try to make a mentor their friend. Recently, a pastor said to me, "Kevin, I want you to know that you have mentored me from a distance." He went on to explain that although we were not close friends and that I didn't know him or socialize with him, he had learned from me. It was a great compliment to me. But perhaps an even greater salute should be given to him for recognizing that God puts people in our lives to fill various roles.

Mentors will not always be friends and contacts will not always be partners. Sometimes people who are great friends decide to become business partners and as result they not only have an unsuccessful attempt to a business adventure, but also mess up what God intended as a life-long friendship. The more people you are able to relate to, the more opportunities you create for God to enlarge you. This is why it's important to develop your ability to relate to a variety of people. Jesus related well to many different kinds of people while remaining selective with his inner circle. His contact list included tax collectors, fishermen, government officials, wealthy people, common people, influential people, doctors and religious leaders.

Make sure that you don't put all of your relational energy into one or two people. When this happens, the people involved end up with limited perspective and unhealthy attachments to each other. Any relationship that causes or requires the exclusion of other relationships is unhealthy. When we only hang out with one or two people excessively, we will fail to experience the value of others that God has put in our lives. *Make it your goal to be friendly and courteous to everyone, but also make it your goal to choose who will and will not have influence in your life.*

A failure to consciously choose will result in the wrong people having influence on you. When you consciously choose, you are "qualifying" people for an influential role in your life. Some relatives are an example of people who may have to be in your life but should not have influence on you. If your family is not going where you want to go in life, treat them with respect and be courteous but don't abandon your course and your goals to fit in with them. Some of the most likable people are not necessarily a positive influence on our lives. These people may be fun or charming to be with, but may not encourage us in our faith or in our role as husbands, wives and parents. There are people that you could learn a trade from but the minute they start to talk about a certain Scripture you may have to remind yourself that they can be a great carpenter but have twisted perspective on the Bible. While you choose that person as a teacher of a trade, you may need to reject their influence in other areas of your life. Your inner circle should be reserved for people you qualify. Here is some criteria I suggest:

1. **Reserve your inner circle for people who are committed to a biblical worldview.** Meaning they govern their choices and behavior by the teachings of the Bible. Make sure that church attendance is not just a religious thing

they do, but a lifestyle they live. Remember, who we are affects who we can have relationship with and whom we have relationship with affects who we are.

2. **Reserve your inner circle for people who bring out the best in you.** When my daughter, Jodi, was learning to play softball, I would pitch the ball where I knew she would swing the bat. By having people who help you get better you will be prepared to face pitching that comes from those who hope you don't get a hit. Our inner circle must be reserved for those whose lives improve and empower us. Bob Richards is the only man to win two Olympic gold medals in the pole vault. When he was trying to break the record held by Dutch Marmerdam, he kept falling short. After trying everything from various coaches to different vaulting methods, he finally called Dutch and asked if he would help him. Dutch became Bob's coach and added eight inches to his best vault. Dutch helped Bob to break his own Olympic record. These are the kind of people you want in your inner circle!

Don't Disconnect from Those
God Has Connected You With

In the story of the prodigal (Luke 15), we see the example of a disconnection initiated by a young man underestimating the effect it would have on his life.

Remember, those who God wants you to be connected to may sometimes disappoint you and wander away from you. Even though the prodigal's father thought his son was making a mistake, he had to let him go. In John 6:66, a crowd walked away from Jesus but he didn't chase them or make house calls asking them to come back. Some people put too much energy into a person who does not want to stay connected to them.

A lack of contentment causes people to disconnect from those that God has connected them to. Even when you are in the right place, you have to work at being content. Some people assume that discontentment is a sign from God that they need to move on to a new spouse, new job or new church. The prodigal, in Luke 15, was in the right place but allowed his own discontentment to move him out of the place he belonged. *When there is a crisis and there is no one there to help, ask yourself, "What relationship did I make the mistake of disconnecting from?"* There are people beating their heads against the walls of poverty and hardship. The only mistake they made was to disconnect from somebody they were to be connected to. Barnabas disconnected from Paul (Acts 15) and we hear very little of him after that.

Irrational thinking and a lack of perspective cause people to disconnect from assigned connections. Only at the bottom of life did the prodigal come to his senses. The loss of perspective blurs the vision of reason and confuses a person's grip on reality. Every day, negativity is magnified and the truth distorted by people who disconnect themselves from assigned connections. You cannot help or restore someone until they are ready to reconnect with their assigned connections. I've found that people who are unwilling to reconnect with their assigned connections never really get out of their "pig pen." Pride keeps some people from reconnecting. They assume that they can abandon relationships without affecting their destiny. Until a person values the God-assigned connection enough to return to it, everything others do for them only sustains them. Their prosperity and future is dependent upon their reconnection to their God-assigned connection.

Four Areas of Relational
Alignment That Impact Your Life Most

1. Your marriage. The kind of person that you marry will have an immeasurable impact on your future. If a woman marries a lazy man, she will live with poverty (Proverbs 10:4). If a man marries a quarrelsome wife, she will be like a constant dripping on a rainy day (Proverbs 27:15). If my wife, Sheila, had married someone else she would probably live in an entirely different city and know different people. If she had married someone not in full-time ministry, her life would be drastically different (Of course, I remind her it would never be as good as it is!)

The mayor of a major city was leaving his office with his wife when a construction worker came over and talked to her. After their conversation ended, the husband asked who he was and how they knew each other. "I almost married him," she said. After walking a few steps down the street the husband said, "Just think, if you had married him you would be living on the salary of a construction worker." The wife said, "No, if I had married him, he would be the mayor of this city!"

2. **Your church.** The church you attend is a relational alignment that will have an impact on your life. Some churches don't expect commitment. Some churches don't challenge a person to improve. There are many styles of churches that have various emphases. The church you connect with will influence your perspective on God. This influence for some has been so negative that they have quit going to church. For others, this influence has been such a positive force in their life that it has literally reshaped the way they think, act and live. Find a church that moves you closer to God and His plan for your life. When you find it – get planted and flourish (Psalm 92:13).

3. Your coworkers. The kind of people you work around is a relational alignment influencing your life. Make it your goal to recognize the influence of those you work with and control its effect on you. If you can't be positive, be neutral, but don't be negative. Every day you will encounter people who disagree, challenge or disturb you. As a result, you may be tempted to react or label people as jerks, creeps or losers. Don't let people "rattle" you or cause a reaction in you. Stay the course as the person you want to be. Typically, the higher you go in any organization the higher quality people you will find. Every coworker can make us stronger and better in one way or another. It's up to us to control their effect on us.

4. Your social ties. These are the people you are with by choice, not by obligation. These are the people we go to movies with, dinners, shopping, golfing, fishing, etc. These are the people we invite into our homes and sometimes hang out with at their house. There is no reason to have social ties with people who don't share your values. In fact, if you have social ties with people whose values are different than yours, you are putting unnecessary stress on your "R&R" time. When there are not shared values, there is pseudo communication, which means you avoid certain topics or subject matters. Also, when there are not shared values there is tension. Social time spent with people who have common values is the optimum use of your "hanging out" time.

Two Are Better Than One
Equals the Power of Agreement

Two are better than one, because they have a good return for their work: If one falls down, his friend can help him up. But pity the man who falls and has no one to help him up! Also, if two lie down together, they will keep warm. But how can one keep warm alone? Though one may be overpowered, two can defend themselves. A cord of three strands is not quickly broken.
—Ecclesiastes 4:9-12 (NIV)

It is not unusual to hear someone say, "I can get more done by myself" or "I'm better off without other people." The truth is we can't and we're not! The above Scripture says:

- Two create a better return for their work.
- Two means there is help in weakness.
- Two means there is warmth in the cold.
- Two can defend themselves better than one.

For some people to think in "agreement" is a total reprogramming of their mind. These people have been programmed to disagree rather than agree. In fact, they interpret agreement as a sign of weakness. The truth is, however, that a soldier is not weak who seeks to live in agreement with his commanding officer. An employee is not weak because he seeks to live in agreement with his employer. A marriage partner is not weak because they seek to live in agreement with their partner.

Nothing that a person can offer a group is more important than an attitude of agreement. A secretary may be able to type two hundred words per minute, but if she can't get along with her coworkers, she will be more of a liability than an asset. When talented singers emerge at our church, if they think more "me" than "we," they can be more of a problem than a blessing. David was approached by a group of skilled and talented warriors (1 Chronicles 12) who asked to be a part of his army. Before David welcomed them he needed to know that they were with him in heart and spirit. Nothing they could offer was more important than an attitude of agreement. *Life's greatest victories are reserved for those who live in agreement.*

In 1988 in East L.A., a nineteen-year-old woman fell asleep at the wheel of her car and drove over a guardrail. The car was left hanging off a bridge by only the left rear tire. Motorists stopped, fire trucks came, tow trucks and rescuers worked for two and a half hours to secure the car enough to make a rescue attempt. After succeeding, a firefighter said the funny part was that in her frustration and impatience, the lady kept yelling, "I'll do it by myself." Fortunately for her, they didn't listen because what one person could not have done, many working together accomplished.

The chairs you sit in, the bed you sleep in, the car you drive, have all been made by a cooperative effort from people. Just one person cannot even make a pencil. The wood comes from a forest in the Northwest. The graphite comes from a mine in South America and the eraser comes from a rubber plant in Malaysia. Thousands of people work together to make a pencil. Two are better than one.

Whether it's in marriage, at church or at work, there will always be opportunities to disagree. The key is to not look for those situations and if you notice them, don't focus on them. Occasionally in our church someone will fuss about a policy they don't like. We have various policies for involvement in ministries such as music, personal workers, or ushers. These policies exist to maintain excellence. An indifferent person would have had difficulty working with Jesus. He gave specific instructions…"take no purse, no bag…no greeting and don't witness outside this region" (Matthew 10).

People who are content to bump along in life can afford to be indifferent, but people who want to be a part of life's greatest victories will live in agreement with others. As Christians, our greatest opportunities are sometimes missed by not living in agreement. Paul told Timothy, "Don't have anything to do with stupid and foolish arguments"(2 Timothy 2:23). Christians have too many stupid and foolish arguments and miss out on the opportunities of living in agreement.

> *"I appeal to you...that all of you agree with one another so that there may be no divisions among you..."*
> —I Corinthians 1:10

> *"How good and pleasant it is when brothers live together in unity."*
> —Psalm 133:1

I think this all adds up to an unarguable Bible theme of living in agreement.

- Get along with others.
- Have a spirit of cooperation.
- Participate with other people in the pursuit of a goal.
- Compromise everything you can for unity.
- Don't be a person who causes strife.
- Don't hang around with divisive people.
- Avoid arguments and quarrels.

Seek agreement, pursue agreement, and live in agreement, because in the place of agreement strength is multiplied. When two separate agencies come together, synergy is created. If one 2 x 4 can support one hundred pounds of weight before breaking, two should support two hundred pounds (mathematically), but in the realm of agreement, synergy is created which multiplies strength. We see this at work in "idea sessions" every day. Individuals, without coming together, all have creative potential. In a "think tank" environment, individual minds synergize and tap into creative power that they are unable to access without coming together. If you take a chair apart, its individual pieces won't even stand up on their own, but together they support the weight of a person. Our individual strength, no matter how great it is, cannot equal the strength created when we join forces as a team.

Think About These Questions:

- What would a guitar be like with only one string?
- What would it be like if you only had your lower teeth?
- What if only one person tries in a marriage?
- What if an ingredient is missing in a recipe?
- What if a computer has a malfunctioning key?
- What if one tire is missing off your car?
- What if one letter is missing from a word (can vs. can't)?
- If nobody had ever made any agreements what would our world be like today?

Famous Quotes

- "None of us are as smart as all of us." (Unknown)
- "There are no problems we can't solve together and few we can solve by ourselves." (Lyndon Johnson)
- "It's amazing what can be done if nobody minds who gets the credit." (Mark Twain)
- "We must all hang together or we will hang separately." (Ben Franklin)
- "You can do what I cannot do. I can do what you cannot do. Together we can do great things." (Mother Theresa)
- "We have not come together to compete with one another, but to complete one another." (Bill McCartney)
- "We should not only use all the brains we have but all we can borrow." (President Wilson)

How to Live With Our God-Assigned Connections

- *"Be at peace with each other."* Mark 9:50
- *"Love one another."* John 13:34
- *"Be devoted to one another."* Romans 12:10
- *"Honor one another above yourselves."* Romans 12:10
- *"Stop passing judgment on one another."* Romans 14:13
- *"Accept one another."* Romans 15:7
- *"Instruct one another."* Romans 15:14
- *"Greet one another."* Romans 16:16
- *"Serve one another in love."* Galatians 5:13

- *"Carry each other's burdens." Galatians 6:2*
- *"Be patient, bearing one another in love." Ephesians 4:2*
- *"Be kind and compassionate to one another." Ephesians 4:32*
- *"Forgive each other." Ephesians 4:32*
- *"Speak to one another with psalms, hymns and spiritual songs." Ephesians 5:19*
- *"Submit to one another out of reverence for Christ." Ephesians 5:21*
- *"In humility consider others better than yourselves." Philippians 2:3*
- *"Teach and admonish one another with all wisdom." Colossians 3:16*
- *"Encourage each other." 1 Thessalonians 4:18*
- *"Build each other up." 1 Thessalonians 5:11*
- *"Spur one another on toward love and good deeds." Hebrews 10:24*
- *"Do not slander one another." James 4:11*
- *"Don't grumble against each other." James 5:9*
- *"Confess your sins to each other." James 5:16*
- *"Pray for each other." James 5:16*
- *"Clothe yourselves with humility toward one another." 1 Peter 5:5*

"Habit"

I am your constant companion.
I am your greatest helper or heaviest burden.
I will push you onward or drag you down to failure.
I am completely at your command.

Half the things you do you might just as well turn
over to me and I will be able to do them quickly and
correctly.

I am easily managed –
You must merely be firm with me.
Show me exactly how you want something done
and after a few lessons I will do it automatically.
I am the servant of all great men; and alas,
of all failures, as well.
Those who are great, I have made great.
Those who are failures, I have made failures.

I am not a machine,
Though I work with all the precision
of a machine plus the intelligence of a man.
You may run me for a profit or run me for ruin – it
makes no difference to me.

Take me, train me, be firm with me,
and I will place the world at your feet.
Be easy with me and I will destroy you.
Who am I? I am habit!

(Anonymous)

CHAPTER FOUR

THE FORCE OF HABITS

Great people have *great* habits. The people we admire most for their character and achievements are people with great habits. These people have learned how to harness the power of habit and use it effectively.

- Jesus had a habit of going to the church every Sabbath. (Luke 4:16)
- Daniel had a habit of giving thanks to God in prayer three times every day. (Daniel 6:10)
- David had a habit of praising God continually. (Psalm 34:1)

Nobody is going to compete in the Olympics without first embracing a lifestyle of habit. Champions have champion habits. If you want to rise above mediocrity…if you want to create a positive force that will move you towards a dream…habit is the choice of champions.

First We Make a Habit, Then a Habit Makes Us

Larry Bird, the great Hall of Fame NBA superstar, was filming for a commercial when he was asked to miss one of his famous jump shots without changing his shooting form. His shooting form was not like someone who goes out and plays a basketball game in their driveway and shoots different every time they shoot. Larry Bird's form was a fine-tuned rhythm that his fans had seen consistently over his career. He was literally like a shooting machine. The producer of the commercial waited patiently for Larry to "miss" a shot without changing his form. He shot nine times before missing! He had made a habit and now when asked to miss, his habit of making the shot would not let him miss.

Making and Breaking

There are people who spend all of their time and energy trying to break unwanted habits. If you will stop spending all of your time concentrating on breaking your old habits and instead concentrate on making a new one, then the new habit will break the old one. The new habit will do a much better job of destroying the old habit than you could do on your own. In fact, you need a new habit to break an old one.

New and higher habits can be thought of as:

Healthy	Positive, good for you
Alternative	Options in
Behavior	Conduct, actions that are
Instrumental	Helpful in
Transforming	Bringing desired change
Self	To your life and future.

Not just any alternative will bring positive transformation to your life. A healthy alternative is needed to replace an unhealthy behavior pattern. Psychologists say it takes an average of twenty-one days to develop a habit. In other words, you can't do something a couple of times and expect to do it naturally from then on. When you decide to implement a new behavior into your life it will take time before it becomes a pattern. It's like having your phone number changed. The automatic thing to do is to pick up the phone and call the old number. You have to catch yourself, stop the process, and replace the old habit with a new, strange number. It feels awkward at first. Your old habit resists the new number being logged in the mind's status of "home number." Only by repeated and conscious effort do you implement the new number into the memory as your home number. Once it is there however, you will again be able to grab a phone and automatically dial the new number.

Healthy alternative behavior can only become comfortable, easy and automated after repeated and conscious effort on your part. Eventually, however, your new healthy habit will come naturally. Once this happens the old negative habit is replaced and eliminated. This is where many people make a major mistake when they want to make a positive change. They concentrate all their energy on breaking the unwanted habit. They think of the unwanted habit as being strong, deeply rooted, and unmovable. They see the staying power of the negative habit and feel incapable of breaking it. As a result, they usually experience defeat. On the other hand, if we focus on forming a new, positive habit we are more likely to concentrate on the benefits of this new habit. We will see the strength it will bring to our lives and become more motivated. The new habit should be an alternative to the old, and by making the new habit we will automatically break the old one. We don't have to worry about breaking it – the new habit will break the old one. Again, everyone lives with habits and the object is not to be free of habits, but to be free of negative habits and in the routine of higher habits! With a higher lifestyle you will probably have more habits, but they will be healthy ones. Every real winner in life succeeds with the discipline of healthy habits!

The people who know you well (family, friends, and coworkers) know your habits. In fact, people associate what kind of person we are with the habits we have.

- Some people are always late, while others are never late.
- Some people always see the problems while others always see the possibilities.
- Some people are predictable "frowners" while others are predictable "smilers."

Once we form a habit we continue in it until we make a conscious effort to change. Author Catherine Marshall told of a time in her life when she sensed God telling her to go on a "fast" from criticism. For one day her assignment was to not criticize anybody about anything. She wrote, "For the first half of the day, I simply felt a void, almost as if I had been wiped out as a person. This was especially true at lunch...I listened to the others and kept silent...that afternoon, a specific, positive vision for life was dropped into my mind...ideas began to flow in a way I had not experienced in years. My critical nature had not corrected one single thing…what it had done was stifle my own creativity."

When You Change Habits, by Improving Them, You Literally Change and Improve Your Life.

Every day, all of our lives are shaped and directed by the force of our own habits. We are what we repeatedly do. A person is not friendly because they were friendly once. Likewise, a person is not unfriendly because they were unfriendly once. A person isn't a coffee drinker because they drank it once. Coffee drinkers drink coffee repeatedly. *When what you do repeatedly changes, your life changes.*

A change of habit…

- Can qualify you for a career promotion.
- Can open the door for new and better relationships to enter your life.
- Can increase and position you in a place of prosperity.
- Can cause people to respond more eagerly to you.
- Can change the atmosphere in your home.
- Can deepen and strengthen your relationship with God.
- Can add years to your life and increase the quality of your life.

Imagine yourself as an employer and one of your employees is always pointing out problems and asking you for help. Another employee is always solving problems for themselves and other staff members in your company. You respond to these individuals differently; not because of their age, gender or skin color, but because of their habits. One of them is a burden in your mind and the other one is a blessing in your mind—for no other reason except, habits. In much the same way, people are responding to you, not based on your intentions but your habits. A simple habit of always being late can cause others to feel that you disrespect their time by making them wait on you to arrive. If offensive habits go unnoticed or unchanged in a person's life, it will limit the quality and health of otherwise great relationships. On the flip side of the coin, a person who recognizes and changes their own annoying, negative habits, makes themselves a candidate for the admiration and appreciation of others.

Other lifestyle habits that change our lives when we change them are:

- Our spending habits
- Our driving habits
- Our social habits
- Our talking habits
- Our dressing habits

- Our eating and drinking habits
- Our giving habits
- Our reading habits
- Our church attendance habits
- Our exercise habits

Keep on Adding

Ask yourself, "If I could change one habit, what would I change?" Whatever the answer is, that's where you should begin alternative behavior. Don't try to become faultless or perfect in the next three days. Focus on one mannerism, one personality glitch, or one character flaw. Make every effort to add to who you already are as a person.

> *...make every effort to add to your faith, goodness; and to goodness, knowledge; and to knowledge, self-control; and to self-control, perseverance; and to perseverance, godliness; and to godliness, brotherly kindness; and to brotherly kindness, love. For if you possess these qualities in increasing measure, they will keep you from being ineffective and unproductive in your knowledge of our Lord Jesus Christ.*
> *—2 Peter 1:5-8*

Notice, the adding of positive habits will keep you from being ineffective and unproductive. Some people get satisfied with who they are. They see no point in adding anything new to their life. They have a job, a spouse and now they are in the "coasting" time of their life. No more "climbing" for them, that would require too much effort! What these people fail to realize is that everything is changing whether we like it or not. If we are not making positive changes, then negative changes are making us! You either grow or decay. That's why Peter is telling us here to take the initiative and make every effort to add positive habits to our lives.

I have watched some so-called "old-time" Christians who just don't want anything new. They want to keep everything predictable, like it has been for twenty years. However, God wants both young and old to never stop learning and never stop growing. He wants them to keep finding ways to add to their strength, and avoid stagnation by their continual forward motion. Some people keep wondering when pastors are going to go on to "new revelations," while many pastors are wondering when some people are going to apply the revelations they have already been taught. It's not what you hear that makes you productive, it's what you do!

"Do not merely listen to the word, and so deceive yourselves. Do what it says."

—James 1:22

In the sports world, the purpose of a coach is to point out what an athlete needs to do to become a better athlete. In the game of baseball, for example, you must learn to do several things well. The development does not all come at once. When my daughter Jodi began playing softball she first had to get comfortable with the equipment. Then she began the continual process of improving all of her skills. It's not enough to be able to catch a ball; she also works on her hitting. Then that's still not enough— she gets me out in the yard to play catch in order to improve her throwing. Because she has the desire to be good, she pays close attention when her coach and dad tell her what to work on. Even champions don't outgrow the need for a coach to help them increase their skill level. Champions welcome the words of a coach who says things like, "get the bat off your shoulder" or "you better work on your throws." A champion knows that when they stop making every effort to improve, their performance will go downhill. The principle is clear. The principle is real. It is true in every area of your life. You must keep adding new healthy habits to stay effective and productive. You must have that whatever-it-takes attitude to accomplish your goals in life.

Old Habits Hinder New Life

I don't know what habits you brought with you when you became a Christian, but I can tell you that old habits hinder new life. The worry habit, the anger habit, the gossip habit, the hanging out with old friends habit, the cursing habit, the fighting habit, the drinking habit, the lying habit….(hopefully you're getting the idea). *Old habits hinder new life!* We tend to underestimate the effect that habits have on our lives. So, think of it like this:

- Ten years of complaining versus ten years of thanksgiving.
- Ten years of smoking versus ten years of exercise.
- Ten years of thinking self-defeating thoughts versus ten years of encouraging thoughts.
- Ten years of going to church with a learning attitude (Bible, notebook and pen) versus ten years of going to church out of obligation.
- Ten years of setting goals versus ten years of passive living.
- Ten years of savings versus ten years of excessive spending.

Whenever negative habits are allowed to linger in our lives they steal the possibilities of new and better life. The day that old habits end is the day that a new life can begin.

"To Dream the Impossible Dream"

To dream the impossible dream,
To fight the unbeatable foe,
To bear with unbearable sorrow,
To run where the brave dare not go.
To right the unrightable wrong,
To love pure and chaste from afar,
To try when your arms are too weary,
To reach the unreachable star!

This is my quest, to follow that star,
No matter how hopeless, no matter how far;
To fight for the right–without question or pause,
To be willing to march into hell for a Heavenly cause!!

And I know, if I'll only be true to this glorious quest,
That my heart will lie peaceful and calm,
When I'm laid to rest, and the world will be better
for this;
That one man, scorned and covered with scars,
Still strove–with his last ounce of courage,
To reach the unreachable stars.

(Joe Darion & Mitch Leigh)

CHAPTER FIVE

THE FORCE OF A DREAM

A dream is a vision occurring in a person's soul. We have all been given an inner "picture screen" on which we can see things that we desire for our lives and futures. Some people dream of what it would be like to have a lot of money. Single people dream of what it would be like to be happily married. Students dream of what it would be like to graduate and be finished with their education. Couples dream of owning their own home. Workers dream of being promoted. Weary people dream of going on a vacation. People dream in their cars, in classrooms, in front of a mirror or while laying in bed. The force of a dream is undeniably a force forming our future.

A dream is a faith picture. It's the use of our imagination to envision what we hope and pray for but have not seen. God created our minds to see "pictures." We can see with our mind's eye something different than what we are looking at with our natural eyes. Our lives will gravitate towards the most vivid pictures of our mind. Some of the greatest champions for God were people who had a faith picture for their life.

- *Joshua and Caleb* had a faith picture of the place they wanted to live and raise their children. For forty-five years they envisioned it before they actually experienced it.

- *David and Solomon* shared a faith picture of a temple to be built that would honor God. Their dream became a reality.

- *Nehemiah* had a faith picture of a restored city. He put his heart into his dream and it came to pass.

- *David* knelt at a brook and picked five stones to fight a giant and his brothers. He had a faith picture of his nation winning the war for their freedom.

The Ability to Dream Moves You in the Path of God's Purpose for Your Life

The Lord said to Abram after Lot had parted from him, "Lift up your eyes from where you are

*and look north and south, east and west. All the
land that you see I will give to you and your off-
spring forever. Go, walk through the length and
breadth of the land, for I am giving it to you.*
—*Genesis 13:14, 15, 17*

Notice the instruction of the Lord to Abram.
*"Lift up your eyes...All the land that you see I will give it to
you...Go walk through...the land, for I am giving it to you."*
Abram would not be limited by adversity or opposition,
but would only be limited by what he could not "see. "
God instructs him, *"Go walk around in your future...Get a
feel for its length and breadth."* I remember clearly when I
began to have a "big church" dream in my heart. At that
time a church of one thousand people was "huge."

In fact, none of the churches I attended had over
three hundred to four hundred people. The majority of
the churches were less than one hundred. Whenever I
talked about the church being big, it seemed I always had
somebody rebuking me saying something like, "It's not
the quantity, but the quality that really matters!" My
argument became, "Why not both?" and "Doesn't quality produce quantity?" Later I realized that what those
people didn't know was that God had put a dream in me.
It was His way of bringing His will to pass through my
life. It was very *definitive* and *absolute* in nature. I was
attracted to big churches across the nation to find out

how they became big. I was inspired by a dream that Christian living and the worship of God could be one of the biggest things happening in a city. It wasn't until later years that it became obvious to me that other men and women of my generation were dreaming the same dream. As I look around our nation and world today, it's exciting to see pastors and leaders who don't even know each other, bring forth churches that are marching to the beat of a same drum. This hasn't happened because of an organized effort of man, it's happened because of God-given dreams deposited into people's hearts. On various occasions, I wondered if it was wrong for me to dream. It seemed like I was on a *different page*, singing a *different song* than my denomination. I sometimes wondered *why* am I seeing things so differently than the many church leaders and pastors who seemed comfortable with a small church? Only after time had passed did I realize my ability to dream was a gift from God.

Your dream potential is designed to move you in the path of purpose for your life. Don't doubt it. Don't deny it. It's good…it's right…it's the gift of God.

Dreams Are the Seeds of Reality

In the watermelon seed is a watermelon. Your natural eye can't see it yet because it hasn't been manifested, but it's there. Likewise, a dream is the seed from which reality comes. Look around you today... everything you see began as a dream in somebody's mind.

- The building you're in
- The car you're driving
- The chair you're sitting in
- The flooring beneath your feet
- The fax machine in your office
- The computer at your desk
- The telephone you talk on

These all began as a "dream seed" before becoming a reality. The dreaming that we do when we're awake is a creative seed in the human spirit.

More than six hundred years ago, a Spanish monk by the name of Ramon Lull, was severely beaten while preaching the Gospel to Muslims in South Africa. Two Italians rescued him in a boat and crossed the Mediterranean to his home. While he lay dying, he pointed westward over the horizon and said, "Beyond this sea is another great continent that we've never seen...send men there! Send men there!" One of the Italians was Stefano Columbo, a direct ancestor of Christopher Columbus. The words of this martyr were passed from generation to generation until a dream was born in young Christopher's mind. He spent seven years in the Royal Courts discussing the exploration of the west.

After much opposition, he received the support of Queen Isabella of Spain. Today, we are living in the reality of a nation that was once a dreamland in young Christopher Columbus' heart.

Immigrants run four out of ten Fortune 500 companies, not because they had resources when they started, but because they had a dream.

The Ability to Dream Is a Gift from God

Many believers today have associated meditation and visualization with eastern cults and false religions. Not only was meditation and visualization practiced by our Bible heroes of faith, but it is also a God-given tool of empowered living. Dreams are the mother of ingenuity and living. Pressing in on a dream, to the point that you visualize it and meditate on it, is what God intended for our imagination to do.

Anyone who has ever designed and built their "dream home" will tell you that the process requires the dreamer to imagine rooms not yet built, colors not yet coordinated and lights not yet purchased. When Sheila and I built our home, we spent hours visualizing the next steps of construction so that we could agree on it and guide our builders to build what we pictured in our minds.

Today we enjoy a home that accommodates our unique lifestyle and contains an environment that we created to live in. That ability, to pre-view what we desire for our life and future is one of God's greatest gifts to the human race.

The Will of God Is Like a Circle

I like to think of the will of God as a circle with "options" in it. At the beginning of this chapter we looked at Abraham's dilemma when he and his nephew, Lot's, possessions had outgrown their real estate. A close look at that story (Genesis 13) reveals Abraham's perspective on the change that he and Lot needed to make in order to facilitate the increase they were experiencing. In their discussions they decided to separate with one expanding in one direction and the other expanding in another direction.

Abraham was not hung up on him only having one option within the will of God, but rather he told Lot, "You pick east and I'll go west or you pick west and I'll go east." Abraham was confident that neither of those options would take him out of God's will. He believed he would be blessed whichever way he decided to go. God then encourages him to "Lift up his eyes" and look out at the land before him. Sometimes people get paralyzed by being overconcerned about missing

God's will. This kind of fear shuts down the dreams that faith has called us to envision. People often "spar" with their dreams for fear of doing something outside of God's will. The confusion sounds like this:

- "I want to practice medicine and become a doctor, but what if that's not what God wants?"

- "Our family could use some extra income and my wife would like to go back to work, but I'm not sure that God would want her to do that."

- "There's two great colleges that I'm considering, but I'm not sure where God wants me to go."

In these examples, the focus has gotten off the dream and become confused by what is most likely a matter of personal choice. While we are to pray for God's guidance in our decisions, we are also to have faith that the "circle of God's will" usually allows us options and those options are blessed of the Lord. When God wants something specific from us, He puts it *forcefully* within us and equips us to do it. How we get there is a secondary issue to getting there. So how do you know God's will? Identify your dreams.

As I write this book, my daughter, Jodi, is a college student. Some parents make the mistake of trying to force their kids to live out their (parent's) dreams. Other parents make the mistake of not discussing their children's dreams with them. When you identify the dream within your heart you establish the circle of God's will which can serve as a target for your future.

Desires Are Indicators of God's Will

One of the ways I know my wife was the one for me, was the desire I had to marry her. Isn't it good to know that when God created Eve, Adam liking her and being attracted to her was the intention of God? Think how miserable it could be if God wanted us to marry people that we had no desire to be around. Obviously, there are desires of our flesh which are outside the circle of God's will (1 Peter 2:11). Those desires lead to heartache and loss in our lives. On the other hand, however, there are desires put in us by God that are indications of God's will for our lives (Psalms 37:4, 103:5; Proverbs 10:24).

Medical teams coordinate efforts to get on an airplane and go to a region of the world where doctors and medicine are scarce. These physicians take time off work with no compensation, leave the comfort of home to journey to a faraway place and help people they don't know. Usually these doctors and nurses return repeatedly to war torn and plague-infested lands. The reason they go? Plain and simple—they want to. The good done in a situation like that is only one example of many good things happening every day by people who are inspired to do the desires of their heart. Why am I telling you this? Because many people wrongly assume that God's will is going to be in direct conflict with the desires of their heart.

A Dream Won't Make You Something You're Not, but It Will Make You Everything You Are

A book entitled *Soar with Your Strengths* opens with a parable called, *Let the Rabbits Run*. The parable creates the imagery of a duck, a fish, an eagle, an owl, a squirrel, and a rabbit who decide to become "well-rounded" animals. They put together a curriculum designed to teach them to run, swim, climb trees, jump and fly. By the end of the parable, each animal has tried to do something they were not created and equipped to do. Together, they concluded that the best approach to life would be to have schools and businesses where people are allowed to concentrate on what they do well. A life where rabbits could do nothing but run, squirrels could just climb trees, the fish could just swim, and the duck, the eagle and the owl could be the ones who concentrate on flying.

With a similar message there's a cartoon of a pig with the caption, "Do not try to teach a pig to sing – it will waste your time and annoy the pig."

A dream can't always take a person where they want to go, but a dream can always take a person where they could not go *without* a dream. Many talented musicians have dreamed of being signed by a record company and having a #1 hit who have never attained that goal. However, what they attained by having the dream was more than they would have accomplished without it. Many of them have had great careers in the music industry, made recordings, written songs and maximized their talent. *A dream always benefits the dreamer.* The bonus is when the dream, in its entirety, comes true. In other words, the path to a dream draws out our greatest character and strength. We experience the essence of life when we dream.

"The Path to a Dream"

The path to a dream is paved with sacrifices
and lined with determination.
And though it has many stumbling blocks along the way
And may go in more than one direction
It is marked with faith.
It is traveled by belief and courage

Persistence and hard work.
It is conquered with a willingness
To face challenges and take chances,
To fail and try again and again.
Along the way, you may have to confront
Doubts, setbacks and unfairness.
But when the path comes to an end,
You will find that there is no greater joy
Than making your dream come true.

(Barbara Cage)

What Do You Want?

Jesus asked people He came in contact with, "What do you want? What is it that you want Me to do for you?" Answering this basic question seemed to be a prerequisite to a new beginning in peoples' lives (Matthew 20:21, John 5:6, Mark 10:36, Luke 18:40). Someone jokingly said, "The reason adults ask children all the time, 'What do you want to be when you grow up?' is that they are looking for ideas!" How specific can you be? How familiar are you with where you want to be in two years? Four years? Ten years? Are your dreams held hostage because you're unfamiliar with what you want? More than a few times, I've heard believers answer these very questions with a religious reply of "I want whatever God wants." That's generally another way of saying, "I have *no idea*...not even a clue!" Remember (Genesis 13) God wanted Abraham to "lift up his eyes and look." Until our eyes are lifted and our gaze is fixed on something out there, one of God's greatest gifts is dormant and unused in our lives.

You Can't Hit a Target
If You Don't Have a Target

Once you have determined that a desire is within the circle of God's will, then it's time to decide if you want to make it a target. An archery instructor was in a field, teaching fundamentals of the bow and arrow, when she asked a student who had the bow drawn back to describe everything he saw. "I see the sky, the clouds, I see a tree"...the instructor said, "Put your bow down," and moved to the next student. When asked the same question, that student replied, "I see only a target." "Go ahead," the instructor said, "You're ready to hit the target." Within the circle of God's will, everyone should be able to find the "bull's-eye" of their dreams. Some people see many possibilities. They dream of one thing and then another. Dreaming is effortless for those kinds of people who are natural dreamers. However, these same individuals are the most reluctant to "give up" the dreaming pattern (that they flow so easily in) long enough to focus on a specific dream target and commit themselves to use their time, talent and energy to accomplish the dream.

If what you're looking for in your own life is big enough and your faith to achieve it is strong enough, you will not be distracted by smaller things. When you "lock in" on a dream target, you have no time for small and petty distractions. One person said it like this, "If you're hunting rabbits in tiger country, beware of the tigers...but if you're hunting tigers in rabbit country, don't mind the rabbits." If what you're looking for in your own life is big enough, you don't worry about petty things.

Dreams Fulfilled Are a Tree of Life

"A longing fulfilled is a tree of life."
                                                        —Proverbs 13:12

Many people are unhappy in life today simply because they have unfulfilled longings.

When I entered ninth grade, I knew I wanted to play football. I had no idea what would be required of me so I could ultimately do what I wanted to do. When I showed up at my first summer camp, I had no idea that the next few days of practice in the humid Midwest would be as difficult as it was. In a high school as large as ours, over a hundred boys showed up who thought they wanted to play football. However, by the end of the week, less than fifty remained. Out of that group emerged an even smaller group of guys who embraced the necessary discipline to play Division 4 High School Football. The day I put on my first game uniform, was also my first taste of what it feels like to fulfill a dream. On game days, I was so excited, my adrenaline was pumping, my confidence and self-esteem were sky-high. I had arrived in the place I had dreamed of. I was not just Kevin the student or Kevin the preacher's kid. Those were identities others had put on me. Now I was walking in *my* dream, Kevin the High School football player. It's one thing to fulfill obligations you may have as a parent, employee or Christian. It's an entirely different experience when you fulfill a "longing" of your own heart. Longings unfulfilled make "mad" people, "unhappy" people, "sarcastic" people, while longings fulfilled make life a place of "celebration" and "joy." If you know someone whose life lacks joy, it's likely that there's a trail of unfulfilled dreams in their life. Don't live another day without identifying the dreams God has put in your heart and committing yourself to them. Those longings fulfilled will be a tree of life. I'm ending this chapter with the words to a song written by Lee Ann Womack entitled "I Hope You Dance." This song is a model of encouragement that's not often heard in our society or in our churches. It's an encouragement to push past adversity, take risks and don't pass on your opportunity to pursue your dream.

"I Hope You Dance"

I hope you never lose your sense of wonder
You get your fill to eat but always keep that hunger
May you never take one single breath for granted
God forbid love ever leave you empty-handed

I hope you still feel small when you stand beside the ocean

Whenever one door closes I hope one more opens
Promise me that you'll give faith a fighting chance
And when you get the choice to sit it out or dance

I hope you dance…I hope you dance
I hope you dance

I hope you never fear those mountains in the distance
Never settle for the path of least resistance
Livin' might mean takin' chances but they're worth takin'
Lovin' might be a mistake but it's worth makin'
Don't let some hell-bent heart leave you bitter
When you come close to sellin' out reconsider

Give the heavens above more than just a passing glance
And when you get the choice to sit it out or dance
I hope you dance…I hope you dance
I hope you dance…I hope you dance

I hope you still feel small when you stand beside the ocean
Whenever one door closes I hope one more opens
Promise me that you'll give faith a fighting chance
And when you get the choice to sit it out or dance

Dance…I hope you dance
I hope you dance…I hope you dance

CHAPTER SIX

THE FORCE OF THE
THOUGHTS WE THINK

*Therefore everyone who hears these words of mine
and puts them into practice is like a wise man who
built his house on the rock. The rain came down,
the streams rose, and the winds blew and beat
against that house; yet it did not fall, because it had
its foundation on the rock. But everyone who hears
these words of mine and does not put them into
practice is like a foolish man who built his house
on sand. The rain came down, the streams rose,
and the winds blew and beat against that house,
and it fell with a great crash.' When Jesus had finished saying these things, the crowds were amazed
at his teaching, because he taught as one who had
authority, and not as their teachers of the law.*
—Matthew 7:24-29

As a pastor, I come in contact with people who have great hearts. I've found that a person can have it right in their heart and wrong in their head.

- A person can have the best intentions (heart) and make the worst mistakes (head).
- A person can be sincere (heart) and be wrong (head).
- No amount of faith (heart) will compensate for a bad choice (in your head).

Imagine living in America all of your life and taking your first trip abroad to London. After landing at Heathrow Airport, you rent a car and exit the parking lot by pulling out and driving on the right-hand side of the road. No amount of faith in what you're doing can compensate for the fact that you just made a choice that can lead you to a head-on collision.

As a teenager, I went to youth services and youth camps with young people who had great hearts and great intentions. They experienced God's presence in those young years of their life and wanted to please Him with their lives and future. Today, as I look back, many of those same friends have struggled to live the life they intended to live. Some ended up in jail. Two died of AIDS and many of them have been through painful divorces and unnecessary hardship. Unfortunately, this is the story of many people who have a genuine experience with God, but underestimate the value of a wise and discerning mind.

> *"Wisdom is supreme, therefore get wisdom."*
> —*Proverbs 4:7*

Some people "get it" and some people don't. It's really easy to tell them apart. Those who get it, are enjoying the fruit of wisdom. Those who don't, spend a lot of time confused, frustrated and beating their heads against the wall. The good news is – you can be one of those who get it! You don't have to settle for a life of repeated mistakes. You don't have to be one of the people who make wrong choices. There is a painting that shows the devil at a chessboard with a young man. The devil has just made his move, and the young man's queen is checkmated. On his face is written defeat and despair. One day the great chess genius, Paul Morphy, stood looking at the painting. He studied carefully the position on the board. Suddenly, his face lit up and he shouted to the young man in the paining, "You still have a move – don't give up, you still have a move!" Sometimes we all feel checkmated. It's important to remember that it only takes one word from God…one idea, one new thought to turn the entire situation around.

"If any of you lacks wisdom, he should ask God, who gives generously to all without finding fault, and it will be given to him."

— James 1:5

Notice it says, "Ask God who gives *generously...to all* (without partiality) *...without finding fault* (not condemning our mistakes and ignorance).

This Scripture is God's promise to us that when we ask, He will fill our mind with creative ideas, solutions and right choices. Some people don't pray for wisdom because they assume that it's the same thing as knowledge and education—something they have to go to school for. The fact is that there are people with little education and a lot of wisdom and there are people with a lot of education who have little wisdom. This is why psychologists can write relationship books for couples and themselves have three or four failed marriages, while a couple who barely graduated high school have a great relationship and model family. To the degree that people acknowledge and live in harmony with wisdom, they experience success in life. The reason for this is that when God created the universe, wisdom was the craftsman at his side (Proverbs 8:30). So now, the entire universe functions according to wisdom's ways. Many people assume that success is a product of good luck. In reality, if a person is wise, their wisdom will reward them

(Proverbs 9:12). It does not matter if I plant a seed or if you plant a seed, it will give us the same harvest. Wisdom will produce a great harvest in your life just like it will produce a great harvest in any person's life.

Four Specific Rewards of Wisdom

1. Wisdom is the key that unlocks the favor of the Lord in your life.

"For whoever finds me finds life and receives favor from the Lord."

— Proverbs 8:35

2. Wisdom causes a flow of recognition and promotion to come into your life.

"Esteem her, and she will exalt you; embrace her, and she will honor you."

— Proverbs 4:8

3. Wisdom makes your enemies helpless against you.

"For I will give you words and wisdom that none of your adversaries will be able to resist or contradict."

— Luke 21:15

4. Wisdom brings lasting wealth and prosperity.

"With me are riches and honor, enduring wealth and prosperity . . . bestowing wealth on those who love me and making their treasuries full."

— Proverbs 8:18,21

Wisdom is the foundation of all God's thinking patterns and should be the primary goal of our thought life. Its value in our lives is unmatched by anything else we could desire. With the passing of his father David, Solomon was given the opportunity to request anything he wanted from God. His request for wisdom brought with it the other things that a person of his stature could desire. Favor, wealth, and long life were all a part of the package when Solomon received wisdom from the Lord. When people have problems they usually pray for a miracle. A miracle will get you out of problems, but a lack of wisdom will reproduce the problem.

By praying for wisdom, we can keep ourselves from repeatedly being in a position of urgent crisis. Wise thoughts can keep us from the way of the foolish and carnal mind that leads to repeated sorrow.

Thoughts Are Like Trains,
They Take You Somewhere

"As a man thinks...so is he."

— *Proverbs 23:7*

A person wouldn't think of going to the train station and getting on a train without first checking where the train is going. Many people, however, get on a "train of thought" without ever asking where it's taking them. These people often end up in places they didn't want to go. Places like Angersville, Self-Pity City, Lonesomeville, Poorville, State of Hopelessness...The good news is you can get on a different train of thought and go to Peaceville, Happy Town, Faith City, or State of Courage!! We get, wherever we go in life, on trains of thought. Thoughts make us sad or glad. Thoughts can stress us out or calm us down. Thoughts affect the way we eat, how we sleep, what we wear and who we like. Your thoughts are a powerful force forming your future.

Setting Goals for Your Thoughts

Scripture teaches us to set goals for our thoughts.

And now, brothers, as I close this letter let me say this one more thing: Fix your thoughts on what is

true and good and right. Think about things that are pure and lovely, and dwell on the fine, good things in others. Think about all you can praise God for and be glad about.
— *Philippians 4:8 (The Living Bible)*

I find it helpful to set goals for my thinking in two specific areas. First in the area of my concepts and secondly in the area of my focus.

- Concepts = Thinking right about things
- Focus = Thinking about right things

1. **Concepts** – In the last couple of years, books have appeared in bookstores with titles like, *Leadership for Dummies, Finances for Dummies, Ten Stupid Things Men Do, Ten Stupid Things Women Do.* My friend, Holly Wagner, wrote a book for couples entitled *Dumb Things She Does, Dumb Things He Does.* Ironically, these books have attracted readers and sold well because people realize that a lot of our problems in life are based on faulty thinking concepts. People are hungry for concepts that will produce better results in their future. People want to know "What is it that I'm thinking wrong about?" "How can I not be so stupid next time?"

I'm greatly encouraged when I see the concepts of the Bible appearing in secular places. Self-help books, business magazines, training seminars and relationship experts are all pointing people towards the concepts of Scripture, concepts like commitment, integrity, giving, goal-setting, monogamous relationships and consideration of others. There seems to be a growing awareness that not all thinking is right thinking and that good concepts are essential to a successful life. I try to check my concepts and make sure that the way I'm seeing a situation is the right way to look at it. It's amazing how you can get different perspectives on a situation, if you take the time to and are willing to seek it. This is one of the benefits of being around successful people. You can hear their concepts and upgrade your own concepts from coach to first class.

2. **Focus** – Imagine that you're seated in a fine restaurant and a waiter is approaching your table. Before he arrives, let me give you some background on his day, so far. Just as he was leaving his home to come to work, the bank called and informed him that his account was overdrawn. They told him that he must make a deposit immediately to keep from being charged for bounced checks. Grabbing his checkbook and coat, he rushes to the car so he can stop by the bank and still get to work on time. It's raining outside and as he gets in his car he drops his waiter jacket on the wet pavement. Traffic is heavy and he's late getting

to work. Now…knowing this background, how do you expect this frustrated waiter to approach your table? Is it okay with you if he is unfriendly? Impatient? Complains to you about his day? Or do you expect this frustrated waiter to greet you with a smile and be pleasant and helpful as he serves you? Of course we expect the latter and so does his employer. In fact, by changing his focus and providing good service, he will not only make his boss happy, but also get some generous tips from happy customers. Changing focus is something people do every day. It's something we expect others to do and should never doubt our own ability to do it. Learning to change your focus will produce tremendous rewards in your life. On any given day, we could all choose to focus on something in our lives that would cause us to be discouraged. By choosing to focus on the things described in Philippians 4:8, we create a better and more encouraging life for ourselves.

Nothing Changes Until
We Change the Way We Think

"Don't accept an invitation to eat a selfish persons' food, no matter how good it is. People like that take note of how much you eat. They say, 'Take all you want!' but they don't mean it."
— Proverbs 23:6-7 (Contemporary English Version)

This Scripture is the modern and expanded version of *"As a Man thinketh, so is he..."* (Proverbs 23:7) and is literally describing a selfish person who puts on behavior to impress others, but makes no adjustment in their thinking. The writer is saying that if a person thinks selfish thoughts, they may camouflage it with unselfish words, *but unless they change the way they think, they remain selfish.* It's interesting to me that the writer says, "Don't eat their food"...who they are hasn't changed by what they say.

In Steven Covey's Book, *The Seven Habits of Highly Effective People,* he describes the blurred line between what he calls personality ethics and character ethics. The point that he makes is that while we place emphasis on the development of personality (gestures, smiles, courtesy), we should never assume that those skills are the same as character ethics (principle guided beliefs).

Much like the selfish person we read about in the above Proverb, many people put on behavior to be well thought of by others, but make no adjustments in the way they think. The result is that they can be the person they want to be temporarily, but not permanently. Employers often wonder after hiring someone where that person they interviewed disappeared to. Youth pastors often wonder what happened to the young person who showed such commitment at summer camp and now that school has started, doesn't even show up at youth service. The fact is that people are all a product of their thinking. Nothing defines us like our thoughts. If the way a person thinks doesn't change, they don't change. Mental ruts are deep and although we can temporarily drive outside the ruts (to make necessary impressions on others) our thoughts will pull us back into the ruts. Only the renewing of our minds will bring transformation to our lives (Romans 12:2).

As I put the phone to my ear, I heard the sobbing man's voice on the other end attempting to inform me that he had returned home from work to find a note from his wife saying that she and the kids were gone – this time for good. Michael had fallen into the same behavior patterns repeatedly, and although he promised each time to change, he always ended up back in the same place. We had prayed together. He had repented numerous times to both God and his wife. He had never stopped attending church, but that wasn't enough to keep him from ending up in the same place he had vowed he would never go again. Until a person becomes selective on their "train of thought," nothing changes. An angry person can pray and receive prayer, but if they still get on the train of angry thoughts, nothing changes. A critical person can say they are sorry, but if they still think critical thoughts they will be critical again. A negative person can pray for faith, but unless they intentionally change the way they think, they will continue in negativity. I believe that going to church is a way of life for Christians. However, if attendance doesn't change the way a person thinks, it won't change the person. The only way to get different results and go to new places in your life is to renew your mind with new and better thoughts.

Thinking New and Better Thoughts Changes Who We Are

A major part of our identity is wrapped up in the way we think. To change our thinking is an admission that who we have been is not the person we want to be. When I walked into a diet center, fifty pounds over-weight, they immediately confronted my thinking about food and exercise. Coming from a family of big eaters, whose social life had been built around eating, we had thought of food as the best and most exciting part of every day. I could not imagine life without high-fat and starchy foods. I never liked salads and vegetables and (although I wouldn't admit it) the thought of exercising had not entered my mind since high school. I had a rep-utation to uphold with people who were like me. We had ordered big pizzas together, gobbled down fast food together and laughed about the relaxed muscles that were "drooping" all around our bodies. Sure enough, when that circle of friends realized I was trying to change, they gave me little encouragement. This change meant I would not be who I had been. To identify me as a person who didn't care about what I ate would not be accurate. To identify me as "Eat Drink and Be Merry Kevin" would now be an inaccurate representation of who I was becoming. A portion of my identity was wrapped up in the way I thought about food and exercise. The point I want to emphasize here is that *thinking new thoughts can be an unsettling experience because it literally changes who we are.*

Many people won't embrace new thoughts because new thoughts make them a different person. Some people are connected by a common tendency to make bad assumptions. They have built their relationships discussing what they assume is going on in the neighborhood or the church or the nation. As soon as one of these people decides to stop assuming the worst about everything and begins to think better thoughts, they jeopardize their friendships. The friend notices the change and may even attempt to tell others, "She has really changed—we used to get along great, but now she's so different"…(of course, throwing in some assumptions!) New thoughts create a new you, and as a result change the way you see yourself and others see you. When you "upgrade" your thinking, you create a common ground with people who tend to think "upgraded" thoughts and embrace life at a new level.

The Power of Internal Dialogue

A young man named Jason, worked on a train crew as a mechanic. He was healthy, had many friends, but was a notorious worrier. One summer day, the train crew was informed they could quit an hour early. The crew began picking up their tools and preparing to go home. Accidentally, Jason was left locked in a refrigerated boxcar. Realizing what had happened, he shouted and banged on the door, but no one noticed. Jason began to worry, thinking to himself, "If I don't get out of here, I'll freeze." He found a rusty screw lying on the floor and began using it to etch words on the wall of the boxcar. He wrote, "It's so cold, my body is getting numb. These may be my last words." The next morning, the crew slid open the heavy doors of the boxcar and found Jason lying unconscious on the floor. The crew quickly rushed him to the hospital. Later it was found that Jason's physical signs showed that he had suffered from hypothermia. When the crew returned to the sight, they discovered that the refrigeration unit of the box car was inoperative, and the temperature inside was fifty-five degrees. Jason's fear and worry had changed his physiology and he made himself sick through the power of his own thoughts. Although this story may seem extreme, no one who studies the effect that our internal dialogue has on us underestimates its power. Most of us have experienced sweat and rapid heartbeat as our body responds to a thought...real or imagined. In other instances, snake bite victims have died when there was not enough poison in them to have killed them. In a much more common experience, we identify a person's internal dialogue by their posture, facial expressions and words. My point is that thoughts are so powerful that they impact our lives physically, spiritually, and emotionally. When under mental stress, people experience change in their sleeping habits, eating habits, and overall outlook on life. This is all triggered by an "internal dialogue" of worry and fear. By changing the "internal dialogue," a person can literally reprogram their mind and change their life experience. Scripture tells of a woman who came to see Jesus for healing and had been hemorrhaging for twelve years. This woman had an internal dialogue of faith (Matthew 9:21) that she was going to be healed. That internal dialogue moved her into position to receive a miracle.

Another example of internal dialogue affecting a person's life, can be seen in the parable of the talents (Matthew 25:25). The inner voice causes one person to fear losing his talent – he buries it; while another person's internal dialogue causes him to multiply and increase what he had been given. What we're looking at in this parable is different behavior resulting from different internal dialogue. We see it every day. One person's fear is another person's ambition. What may cause discouragement for one person, can draw out the fight in another person.

CHAPTER SEVEN

THE FORCE OF FEELINGS

The Spirit Of Our Minds

"And be constantly renewed in the spirit of your mind [having a fresh mental and spiritual attitude]..."
— *Ephesians 4:23 (Amplified Version)*

"The spirit of your mind" in the above reference indicates a mental mood or frame of mind. This Scripture implies that everyone is susceptible to what we know as "mood swings." It further instructs us that if we are going to avoid the damaging influence of a bad mood, we should constantly be renewing the spirit of our minds. It's safe to also conclude that this *Scripture is telling us that without renewal, the spirit of our minds will, by nature, stoop low...* as if pulled by nature's gravity to feelings of self-pity, hopelessness, fear, anxiety, worry, sadness or frustration. Learning the value of renewal and learning the way to renewal can protect us from the unproductive and sometimes destructive behavior that a bad mood will cause in our lives.

Circumstances affect the mood of our minds on a daily basis.

- The alarm clock doesn't go off and makes us late for work.
- Roadwork causes detours around construction and slow moving traffic jams.
- We get halfway to our destination and remember something we forgot at home.
- The school nurse calls and says your child isn't feeling well and you have to cancel an important meeting to go pick up your child.
- We were drinking a latte when it suddenly ended up on our lap.

These are just examples of the many circumstances that affect the mood of our minds on a regular basis. No wonder this Scripture encourages us to be *constantly renewed* in the spirit of our mind!

Our "mood of mind" is not a sin, but it can lead to sin. We've all done things because of a "mood of mind" that we regretted later.

- Every day a child is slapped, because of a mood of mind.
- Every day a good job is lost, because of a mood of mind.
- Every day someone curses God, because of a mood of mind.
- Every day someone gets drunk, because of a mood of mind.

An even deeper concern is appropriate when "a mood of mind" becomes a "stronghold of the mind." This happens when we don't renew the spirit of our mind out of its temporary mood and the mood settles into a permanent condition of mind.

The weapons we fight with are not the weapons of the world. On the contrary, they have divine power to demolish strongholds. We demolish arguments and every pretension that sets itself up against the knowledge of God, and we take captive every thought to make it obedient to Christ.
— 2 Corinthians 10: 4,5

Notice the explanation for strongholds, "...arguments... pretensions and thoughts...." Imagine our petty argumentative moods…our pretensions and thoughts…becoming "strongholds." The biblical meaning of the word stronghold is "a fortified, well-protected dwelling." In this reference, it appears the writer is saying that our arguments, pretensions and thoughts can become so much a part of our minds that only a battle using spiritual weapons (the Word, prayers, faith and confession) can cause them to break down and surrender to the higher thoughts taught in God's Word.

Mood Management

The control of your feelings by way of renewal is what I refer to as mood management. To over-spiritualize this will cause a person to overlook practical and proven methods of renewal. To deny the spiritual implications of a mood of mind is to create superficial, shallow change, rather than genuine internal transformation.

> *Do not conform any longer to the pattern of this world, but be transformed by the renewing of your mind. Then you will be able to test and approve what God's will is – his good, pleasing and perfect will.*
> *– Romans 12:2*

Therefore, we should seek mood management as having spiritual significance although we approach it in a practical manner. Some of the most common moods of mind that need continual renewal are listed below.

1. **The Angry Mood of Mind** – This mood of mind includes feelings of being mildly irritable to being enraged. Anger is something we are allowed to feel momentarily. It is, however, a nonproductive feeling which can cause us to self-destruct, not to mention abuse or hurt others in the process. Proper mood management will quickly transition anger into a more productive feeling by confronting our thoughts with questions like:

- What can I learn from this?
- Is it possible I'm making matters worse by being angry?
- Is there something I may not know or be aware of that would cause this?
- Is this merely a misunderstanding that good communication could remedy?

The Bible says: *"Good sense makes a man restrain his anger, and it is to his glory to overlook a transgression or an offense"* (Proverbs 19:11 Amplified Version). Another Scripture says: *"...do not let the sun go down while you are still angry"* (Ephesians 4:26). In other words, "be renewed in the spirit of your mind" before you go to bed at night.

2. **The Troubled Mood of Mind** – This is what you feel when you *don't understand* something that is important to you. Like all feelings, if not dealt with, they can intensify. A positive adjustment to a *troubled* mood of mind is to disarm the threat of what you don't understand. There will always be some questions unanswered. The need to understand is a God-given curiosity that can produce knowledge and growth in us. It's when the curiosity escalates and we *fear the unknown* that our mood of mind will shift into a troubled mind. This shift happened as Jesus was describing the future to His disciples. He evidently sensed that some of them were allowing the unknown to be a source of inner turmoil. His guidance to them was, *"Do not let your hearts be troubled…" (John 14:1).* The message was a compelling "take charge of your feelings" message… *"do not let…"* was a clarification of our responsibility to forbid the access of troubled feelings into our hearts.

3. **The Discouraged Mood of Mind** – To be discouraged is the condition of lacking courage, hope, and confidence. Discouragement is an enemy opposing our faith, prayers, good works, relationships, and joy. There are seven reasons why people get discouraged:

- People get discouraged when there are too many demands on their time.

- People get discouraged when they feel misunderstood.
- People get discouraged when they feel powerless to change an undesired circumstance.
- People get discouraged when they are drained by the needs of others.
- People get discouraged by feelings of insignificance.
- People get discouraged when they feel that they have failed.
- People get discouraged by repeated hardship.

This feeling can be triggered by both real and imagined incidents in our lives. Its severity ranges from "blue" feelings to clinical depression. One of the greatest opponents of discouragement is action. As in most situations, renewal comes by doing the exact opposite of what we feel like doing. The discouraged mood of mind causes us to feel a need to withdraw and be inactive. In many neighborhoods there are homes where the lawn is unkempt, there is clutter in excess, the paint is chipping, etc. It's not because the homeowner doesn't have time, in fact they spend most of their time inside the house eating and watching TV. That's exactly what they *feel* like doing. The more they withdraw the harder it is for them to be proactive. The remedy is to counteract the destructive feeling of withdrawal and inactivity by becoming active, social and productive. A prophet named Elijah was discouraged in 1 Kings 19. The angel that God sent to help him ordered him to "get up and get going...." Come out of isolation, reconnect with people and be active.

We could go on with other feelings that slip into our lives on a regular basis. They are numerous and different for everyone. The important purpose of this chapter is not accomplished by merely continuing to describe these feelings. Although we like to know that someone else can relate to our "moods," the real goal must be to learn mood management as a practical means of renewing the spirit of our minds on a *daily* basis. Things I do and recommend to you are listed below.

Stay aware of your feelings. Sometimes people don't stay conscious of how they feel. When you identify your feelings, you then can consider what you need to do to connect a wayward mood of mind. In Psalm 42:5, David asked, *"Why are you downcast O my soul? Why are you so disturbed within me?"* He then proceeds to have a conversation with himself, encouraging his soul to "put hope in God," and declaring that praise will continue to be in his mouth. How many times do people feel moody and make it worse by describing the way they feel (to anyone who will listen), rather than identifying it as only a temporary feeling that they will not give in to? Monitor and manage your mood.

Be honest about your feelings. This does not mean *announce* your feelings. When a person thinks being honest about how they feel means announcing how they feel, they only *affirm* by their words that *unwanted* feeling in their life. What I mean by being honest is aimed at being honest with yourself. Denial of a feeling will only permit it to remain in you. It is easy to do this denial routine when we don't want to *claim* a negative feeling as our own. Feelings like fear, jealousy and inferiority are difficult to admit to having. Self-admission, however, allows us to pray forgiveness and speak renewal over our heart and mind.

Listen to uplifting and inspirational music. Music is a source of inspiration that can encourage and lift our spirits. When King Saul was depressed he would call for David to come and play the harp for him. It's amazing, if you observe at Christmastime how the holiday music has a lifting effect on everyone. Music doesn't have to be limited to holidays and church services. It can be a part of your daily life. My wife and I are constantly looking for new refreshing music that inspires us to praise God, count our blessings, stay in love, and expect the best for our future.

Listen to positive and compelling speakers. Our knowledge increases and our faith grows by hearing (Romans 10:17). The time we spend in our automobiles is the perfect opportunity to listen to audio tapes of church services, conferences and seminars. You will find that your automobile can host God's presence and is a great place to renew the spirit of your mind each day. If you are a business manager or owner you can access great motivation from some of the world's greatest communicators by audio tape. If you have specific business concerns or needs, they can be addressed and supplied every day through listening to knowledgeable speakers. The spirit of my mind has been renewed countless times by listening to positive and compelling speakers on audio tape.

Monitor your energy level. At no time are we more vulnerable to negative feelings than when we are drained of our energy. Energy can be created by regular exercise and good eating habits. God created our bodies for physical activity. In the age of automobiles and computers, our lifestyles don't demand physical exertion. This lack of activity causes a buildup of dead cells and toxic material in our bodies. The only way to keep this "deadness" moving out of you is with deep breathing and muscle movement. How we feel is so closely related to our energy level that we must create and restore depleted energy every day. I've found that giving myself permission to play serves as a source of protection against energy drain. I sometimes joke that a "good round of golf keeps the devil away."

Surround yourself with the right people. The people you spend time with will affect the mood of your mind. Some people are very "resourceful" people and others are very "draining" people. All of us must learn to cope with a certain amount of needy people in our lives, but none of us should spend an excessive amount of time with those who deplete our energy. Jesus had relationships on three levels of interaction.

- *The Crowd* – were the people He ministered to and exchanged courtesy with. This was His community of acquaintances and His fellowship of believers.

- *The Twelve Disciples* – were the friends He socialized with and interacted with more frequently. He had meals at their house, kicked off His sandals in their living room and felt very comfortable with them.

- *The Three Closest Disciples* – were the ones he pulled aside to be closest to (Peter, James, and John). They interacted at a "best of friends" level. It's my observation that these three were protective of Him and He had a special chemistry with them that was good for Him. Peter was full of courage, John was young and energetic, and James was a pillar of faith.

Just like Jesus needed to surround himself with the right people, we also need to make sure that we're aware of how people affect us and surround ourselves with the "right" people. When depressed, many people withdraw, pull the shades and pretend nobody's home. Studies show, however, that when people socialize about 82 percent of the time they reported being in a better mood. With that in mind – seek out those positive people who reinforce your *values* and spend time surrounding yourself with them.

Build yourself up in faith. *"But you dear friends, build yourselves up in your most holy faith and pray in the Holy Spirit" (Jude 20)*. Since feelings originate in thoughts, faith-filled thoughts can create "feelings of faith." This Scripture teaches us to assume responsibility for building ourselves "up" in faith. As you stay aware of your feelings, you can know when you need to build yourself up. Don't wait for someone else to encourage you. Go ahead and encourage yourself! Your prayers should include positive declarations of self-worth and purpose in your life. David continually praised God for His provision of strength in his life. He said things like:

- *"I am fearfully and wonderfully made..."* (Psalm 139:14)
- *"Though war be all around me, I will be confident..."* (Psalm 27:3)
- *"The Lord delights in the well-being of His servant..."* (Psalm 35:27)
- *"As we delight ourselves in the Lord He gives us the desires of our heart"* (Psalm 37:4)
- *"In my integrity you uphold me"* (Psalm 41:12)

You too can manage moods by building yourself up in faith. This will help secure you against feelings that can affect your future in a negative way.

"Lighten Up" – The Spirit of Your Mind

Most of us have a scale that is intended to tell us how much we weigh physically. It can be surprising to step on a scale and realize you've put on some extra pounds. Wouldn't it be great if we had a scale that could weigh our spirit and tell us when we're too "heavy"? Just like we put our bodies on a diet to shed those extra, unhealthy pounds, our spirit can also benefit from a "lightening up" effort.

- When life is all work and no play…it's time to lighten up.
- When laughter is an uncommon sound…it's time to lighten up.
- When there's no celebrating life…it's time to lighten up.
- When praise is an unfamiliar language…it's time to lighten up.
- When you only see the bad…it's time to lighten up.

My greatest concern in being called to the ministry was that I would be pressured to live within the stereotype life of the clergy…and I didn't want to be what most clergy were cloned into being. The vows of celibacy and poverty were not my idea of the more abundant life (John 10:10)! Most "men of the cloth" are expected to wear drab clothes and look like they held a night job at the mortuary. The same seems true for the stereotypical perspective of being a Christian. Christians are assumed to only think about serious matters and resign themselves to a life of heaviness. The stereotype says Christians don't party, don't like any music except organ music, have boring irrelevant services, frown on having fun, have no personal ambitions, dislike people who are not Christians, always wear outdated clothes, and frown on people who want to make more than a moderate income. Unfortunately, many Christians perpetuate this stereotype and society assumes all Christians are living a life of bondage and heaviness. Jesus, on the other hand, offered to help people "lighten up."

> *Come to me all you who labor and are heavy-laden and overburdened, and I will cause you to rest. [I will ease and relieve and refresh your souls.] Take my yoke upon you and learn of Me, for I am gentle (meek) and humble (lowly) in heart, and you will find rest (relief and ease and refreshment and recreation and blessed quiet) for your souls. For My yoke is wholesome (useful, good - not harsh, hard, sharp, or pressing, but comfortable, gracious, and pleasant), and My burden is light and easy to be borne.*
> *— Matthew 11:28-30 (Amplified Version)*

The choice to "lighten up" is a step of faith. Have you ever heard someone say, "I want to be happy, but I can't"? Faith says, "I won't let my problems weigh me down, discourage me, or keep me from being happy." I can almost hear someone saying right now, "If life's a bowl of cherries, why am I always in the pits?" The truth is – life's not a bowl of cherries. Hardly a week goes by in our ministry without someone we know reporting a crisis. A financial, relational, or health crisis is always in the neighborhood of our lives and sometimes right smack in the living room.

The most natural thing to do is to allow all of that to steal our joy, consume our thoughts and silence our laughter. Without exception, the people who keep their joy do so by having faith in spite of the fact that life's not a bowl of cherries. Some people stoop low in the mood of their mind by worrying about their age and the passing of time. One senior citizen who is young at heart wrote:

> *Remember, old folks are worth a fortune– silver in their hair, gold in their teeth, stones in their kidneys, lead in their feet, and gas in their stomachs.*
>
> *I have become a little older since I saw you last, and a few changes have come into my life since then. Frankly, I have become quite a frivolous old gal. I am seeing five gentlemen every day.*
>
> *As soon as I wake up, Will Power helps me get out of bed. Then I go to see John. Then Charlie Horse comes along, and when he is here he takes a lot of my time and attention. When he leaves Arthur Ritis shows up and stays the rest of the day. He doesn't like to stay in one place very long, so he takes me from joint to joint. After such a busy day I'm really tired and glad to go to bed with Ben Gay. What a life!*
>
> *P.S. The preacher came to call the other day. He said at my age I should be thinking about the hereafter. I told him, "Oh, I do all the time. No matter where I am – in the parlor, upstairs, in the kitchen, or down in the basement – I ask myself what am I here after?"*

What a great way to lighten up the issue of getting old! Some people let a certain age or birthday start dictating their outlook on life. Even young people sometimes confuse laughter and *fun* with immaturity. Maturity is not the absence of laughter and fun, but a sense of how, when and where to have fun. By all means, make fun a lifetime goal!

If laughter is good for us (Proverbs 17:22) and the joy of the Lord is our strength (Nehemiah 8:10), then surely God wants us to have an ample supply of both in our lives. God's sense of humor is something you don't hear much about. In fact, I'm sure some people don't think He has one. On the contrary, I imagine chuckles and laughter breaking out in heaven just observing a lot of what happens here on earth. It's funny when preachers baptize people three times their size! I know I've put the wrong words together in the pulpit and what came out had to make God smile! I know there's a place and time to be quiet before the Lord and I know there's a time to think sober thoughts, but most Christians I meet today take themselves far too seriously and we can all (including me) benefit by choosing to lighten up the spirit of our minds. I also believe that the strength one needs to serve the Lord can be found by having more fun in church (Nehemiah 8:9-10). It's a fact that laughter increases the body's production of endorphins and serves as the body's natural pain remedy;

so our health will benefit as the natural anesthesia and painkiller of laughter is more a part of our lives (Proverbs 17:22).

Abraham Lincoln, our nation's sixteenth President, was known in his early years as a depressed and melancholy human being. His law partner, William Hearndow, said in 1841 that "melancholy dripped from him as he walked." Note how different he stands in 1863 when President Lincoln, himself, writes, "The year that is drawing to a close has been filled with the blessings of fruitful fields and healthful skies. These bounties are so constantly enjoyed that we are prone to forget the source from which they come." The interesting part about this writing was that he was in the midst of the Civil War when he wrote it, but he was still able to see the good that was around him. Sometime between 1841 and 1863, Lincoln's efforts to overcome a low mood of mind were obviously successful. On another occasion, a member of his staff was trying to get Lincoln to hire a marketing manager that Lincoln refused to hire. When pushed for an explanation, Lincoln simply said, "I don't like his face." The reference was to the lack of smiles and good cheer on the man's countenance. Lincoln had learned to surround himself with people who would lift his spirits. A strategy Lincoln embraced to combat his low moods was to sit with friends before going to bed and tell jokes and laugh. During the Civil War, newspaper reporters criticized him for joking while soldiers were dying. Lincoln's response was to quote Proverbs 17:22, *"Laughter does good like medicine,"* and remind his critics that he was purposely engaging in this practice of "lightening up" so that he could face the heavy burdens of the presidency at such a difficult time.

President Lincoln's approach to managing the mood of his mind is now a commonly believed and accepted therapy called cognitive therapy. The word cognitive simply means thought or perception and cognitive therapy is based on the simple idea that your thoughts, not circumstances, create your moods. By guiding our thoughts we can improve our moods and overcome the feelings that sabotage a life one day at a time.

CHAPTER EIGHT

THE FORCE OF PERSONAL VALUES

As the plane left the gate, I looked out my window and thought to myself, "How is this pilot going to take off in this weather?" I was anxious to get back home, but could not believe how bad the weather was. Outside my window was fog as thick as a blanket. Visibility was so bad I quickly lost sight of the airport as we taxied down the runway. As we took off in the thick clouds, rain, wind and darkness, I thought to myself, I'm so glad we have an instrument panel – a proven system of guidance.

An airplane can be equipped with the best engines and equipment money can buy. It can have reclining seats and great food on board, but if there is not a guidance system that is in sync with a satellite and being guided by a control tower, I don't want to be on board. I don't want to be on a flight without a proven guidance system and I don't want to go through life without a proven guidance system. Just like an airplane needs guidance to reach its desired destination, you and I need guidance to reach our God-planned destiny.

"In those days, Israel had no king; everyone did as he saw fit" (Judges 17:6). Where there's no governing authority...absolute rulership, people do (by instinct, impulse, emotion) as they see fit. This approach to life will result in chaos and self-destruction. On the other hand, the more in harmony people live with the written principles of God, the greater their success. *"...meditate on it day and night, so that you may be careful to do everything written in it. Then you will be prosperous and successful" (Joshua 1:8).*

Making God's Principles Your Values

Values equal whatever you place importance on in your life not what you think should be important to you, but what is important to you.

Everyone is value driven. Salespeople make sales and can convince people to buy when they tap into that person's values. Some shoppers are bargain driven, others are quality driven, and still others are driven by how they feel about the person selling the product.

Values are often associated with good people. The fact is not only good people have values, everyone has values. Gang members, for example, value the acceptance of their gang. Liars are driven by a value of impressing people or protecting themselves. In fact, the only way a person will always be honest, is if honesty is a strong enough value to them.

It's possible to be out of touch with and unaware of your own values. This occurs when something of lesser value, that you're more aware of, is controlling you life. For example, a man or woman can get out of touch with the value they have for their family while a career that actually means less to them is commanding their time and attention. A student can get out of touch with the value they have for their education when distracted by activities that are of lesser value to them. *Unless we stay conscious and aware of our greatest values, things of lesser value can be in the driver's seat of our lives.* Things of lesser value get in the driver's seat, through the doorway of a person's emotions and impulses. Unchecked anger, fear or passion can pull an unguarded individual out of touch with their greatest values.

- A teenage girl afraid to not have sex with her boyfriend.
- A church member dropping out of fellowship with

their church, feeling unappreciated.
- An angry employee, verbally attacking their boss.

All these are examples of people who may be out of touch with their greatest values.

Values can change and when they do – we change. Every time you hear of someone who stopped smoking, lost weight, or changed a negative behavior pattern in their life, you're hearing about someone whose values changed. The person who stops smoking has discovered their value of a healthier, longer life. That discovery brought the change of habit. Likewise, the person who discovers they are tired of not having any money in savings will change their spending habits. Their value change is that they would rather have money in the bank than go shopping for things they don't really need.

If Pleasing God and Succeeding in Life Is a Value to You, the Bible Is a Spiritual and Mental Compass

In the spring of 1999, at San Diego University, twenty-five students were caught cheating on a quiz. It was the worst cheating scandal in the history of the school. The class? Business Ethics! The professors decided to make a permanent record, entered into each student's file, of the incident. The reason they said it was important to the University to make the incident of permanent record was to show that although the students had taken the class, the University's opinion was that they did not apply it. In other words, they rejected it as an instrument of guidance for their life. A Bible principle is much more than religious ideology. A Bible principle is an accurate and sure guide to success in life. One night a massive battleship was cruising coastal waters, when an officer on deck saw the light of an oncoming ship. He summoned the captain and told him of the situation. At the captain's orders, the radio man signaled the oncoming ship: "We are on a collision course. Move ten degrees to the left." Expecting immediate acknowledgement, the captain was surprised to hear the reply, "You move ten degrees." Grabbing the microphone from the radio man's hand, the captain said, "Sir, I am an officer in the United States Navy and commander on this battleship." "Sir," came the reply just as firmly, "I am a lighthouse!" Bible principles are timeless and unchanging laws of life. People argue with them, resist them, and test them. Wise people acknowledge and live by the reliable compass of God's Word. In Chuck Colson's book, *How Now Shall We Live,* he outlines scientific research that supports living according to the biblical moral order is healthier for both individuals and society. There's a growing body of scientific evidence to back up this biblical truth. Medical studies are confirming that those who attend church regularly and act consistently with their faith are better off, both physically and mentally.

Alcohol Abuse: Alcohol abuse is highest among those with little or no religious commitments. One study found that nearly 89 percent of alcoholics say they lost their interest in church during their youth.

Drug Abuse: Numerous studies have found a correlation between spiritual commitment and drug abuse. Among young people, the importance placed on religion is the single best predictor of substance-abuse patterns.

Crime: There is also a strong correlation between participation in religious activities and the avoidance of crime. In one study, Harvard professor Richard Freeman, discovered that regular church attendance is the primary factor in preventing African-American urban young people from turning to drugs or crime. Another study revealed that regular attendance at a Prison Fellowship Bible study cut criminal behavior by two-thirds.

Depression and Stress: In one Gallup survey, respondents with strong religious commitment were twice as likely to describe themselves as "very happy." Armanh Nicholi, professor of psychiatry at Harvard Medical School, argues from his lifelong experience that Christians are far less likely to experience mental disorders. Why? Because "the one essential feature that characterizes all types of depression" is "the feeling of hopelessness and helplessness," and Christians are never without hope.

Suicide: Persons who do not attend church are four times more likely to commit suicide than are frequent church attenders.

Family Stability: A number of studies have found a strong inverse correlation between church attendance and divorce, and one study found that church attendance is the more important predictor of marital stability. It has also shown itself to be an important factor in preventing teen sexual relations, babies born out of wedlock, discord between parent and child, and other forms of family breakdown. Eighty-four percent of strong families identified religion as an important contributor to their strength.

Marital and Sexual Satisfaction: Lest one think these numbers mean that religious people are staying in unhappy marriages from a sense of duty, churchgoers are more likely to say they would marry the same spouse again – an important measure of marital satisfaction. A 1978 study found that church attendance predicted marital satisfaction better than any other single variable. The 1994 Sex in America study showed that very religious women enjoy a higher level of sexual satisfaction in their marriage than do non-religious women.

Physical Health: Studies have shown that maternity patients and their newborns have fewer medical complications if the mothers have a religious affiliation. Belonging to a religious group can lower blood pressure, relieve stress, and enhance survival after a heart attack. Heart surgery patients with strong beliefs are much more likely to survive surgery.

Have the Courage to Trust the Compass

Imagine being on a flight from Los Angeles to Seattle when the pilot comes on the speaker system and informs the passengers that someone on board has suggested that the instrument panel is wrong and that north, as indicated by the airplane's guidance system, is not north. How comfortable would you be entrusting your life to a pilot who is suddenly questioning his proven and accurate guidance system because of something somebody said?

Skilled hikers, climbers, and boaters will choose the guidance of a compass any day over their own instincts. These people all realize how easy it is to get turned around and confused in your sense of direction. *True north*, however, is a fixed and unarguable landmark. The needle of a compass points to the magnetic north pole and communicates to the traveler which way they must journey to go north. Only a fool would argue that what a compass proclaims as north is not *really* north. Only a fool would consider that what was north in 1950 is not *really* north today. The courage to trust the compass brings a person into a place of knowledge and empowers them with direction. They rely on something more absolute than their intuition, feelings or instincts in the journey of life.

> *Do not let this book of the law depart from your mouth; meditate on it day and night, so that you may be careful to do everything written in it. Then you will be prosperous and successful.*
> — *Joshua 1:8*

Our greatest heroes are the people who not only live and have lived from their values, but also had the courage to trust those values in the face of adversity. We are all inspired by those who have the courage to stand for specific values rather than compromise them. We write books about these people and make movies about them. We teach our children to model them. As a kid, I remember watching the classic movie, *It's a Wonderful Life*. Mr. Potter offers George Bailey the job of his dreams in return for closing down his business and giving Old Man Potter the monopoly he needs to charge exorbitant interest on loans. When I was too young to understand the entire plot, I knew Old Man Potter was not being fair and I wanted George to not give in to him. We cheer George on to stand up against the pressure of

Old Man Potter. People like Patrick Henry, Martin Luther King, Jr. and Abraham Lincoln are people that have inspired us with their unwavering commitment to stand by their values in the face of adversity.

- Moses could have had a life of leisure, but chose to be a leader out of loyalty to his people.
- Esther could have remained silent in the suffering of her people, but chose to speak out and take a stand.
- Deborah's courage and deep values brought freedom to an oppressed people.
- Daniel's convictions would not allow him to bow to idols or follow the recommended diet of the king although he was a government official.

These and other Bible characters model for us the force that internal values have on people's lives. The primary reason that there is so much confusion and many misguided choices today is the absence of a spiritual and moral compass in the hearts of people.

Assuming that God's principles are your values, I want to encourage you to live from your values. Here are five keys to help you act in alignment with the principles and universal laws of God.

1. Live from your values, not your hurts, disappointments, or anger. When a person lives from their hurts, they empower them to control and eventually destroy their lives. I listened as Steve Saint stood on our platform and told our church how his missionary father, Nate Saint, was killed by Auca Indians. A few minutes into his story, Steve revealed that the man who was with him was one of the men who had killed his father. You could almost hear the gasp in the crowd, stunned by the fact that this American boy's father had been taken from him and now he was traveling the world and raising money to help the people who had killed his father. If you're going to live from your values, you have to guard your heart (Proverbs 4:23) from the intrusion of life's hurts, disappointments, and anger. These things have a way of causing people to compromise their values. The "takeover" is often unnoticed by the individual themselves, and is justified in their mind because of their unique and difficult circumstances. The determination of Joseph is essential when life isn't fair and others hurt you.

2. Live from your values, not your thirst for approval.

A traveler journeying through the desert came upon a water pump with a note attached. The note explained that buried nearby was a bottle of water. The instructions were to use the water to prime the pump and after getting a drink to leave the bottle filled for the next traveler. Of course, the challenge for the thirsty traveler was to risk pouring out the water in the bottle to prime the pump. What if the pump didn't work? Could the craving and thirst be denied temporarily in order to tap into a greater supply of water for oneself and the next traveler? People who are driven by immediate thirst for approval will typically forfeit values for immediate approval. This immediate gratification costs them the long-term respect and approval that comes to those who delay gratification. For example, a student's thirst for approval can be quenched by the party crowd, or drug and alcohol crowd, by living recklessly and abandoning a sensible, conforming lifestyle. These "live it up" crowds draw in those thirsty for approval. Unfortunately, it costs them the long-term respect and approval of others long after the party has ended. The employer wants to see the college diploma. The lender wants to see their ability to hold a steady job. With nothing but party animal by their name, they forfeit the approval of the employer and the banker.

3. Live from your values, not your natural instincts.

There are two kinds of desires within us. First there are the desires of our heart that God gives us (Psalm 37:4 ; 103:5). Secondly, there are the desires that war against our soul (1 Peter 2:11). When our desires are not consistent with our values or have the potential to bring harm to us or our family, it's a clear indication that the desire is not of God. David made the mistake of sleeping with another man's wife. This one mistake led to an extremely dark and difficult season in David's life. The more he lived from his instincts, the worse it got. His cover up plot made the Monica Lewinski cover up look mild by comparison. Not until David went back to his value led life and resumed a healthy routine that included repentance and church attendance, did he begin to bounce back. David's return to living from his values resulted in him writing some of his best Psalms and leaving a tremendous legacy for future generations.

4. **Live from your values, not your self-imposed limitations.** Consistent church attendance and involvement is a basic value of Christian living. Unfortunately, some people think it is inconvenient or too far of a drive to be 100 percent committed to a lifestyle of involvement in a church. This, of course, is a self-imposed limitation creating conflict with the value of membership in a Christian community. Many of these same people drive a great distance to work every day and think nothing of it. Someone handed me a *Why I Don't Go To Movies* list intended to show how ridiculous and petty the common excuses for not going to church are.

Why I Do Not Go to Movies

- The manager of the theater didn't call me after I attended.
- I did go a few times, but no one spoke to me.
- Every time I go, they ask for money.
- I went so much as a child, I've had all the entertainment I need.
- The thermostat is always too high or too low and the lighting is terrible.
- The movies last too long.

Sound familiar? Self-imposed limitations are governing many peoples lives today, steering them away from their values.

5. **Live from your values, not your awareness of what's wrong with the world.** Don't curse the darkness – light a candle! Many people live as if there is a reward for finding what is wrong with the world.

A story is told of the Secretary of War under Abraham Lincoln, Edwin Stanton, who was well-known for a highly flammable temper. The pressures of war made him easily provoked. On one occasion, he approached Lincoln to complain about a certain general. Lincoln advised him to write the man a letter. "Tell him off," Lincoln responded. Stanton took his advice and promptly wrote a scathing letter in which he directed all his frustration and anger toward the man. He then showed the letter to the President.

"Good," said Lincoln, "First rate. You certainly gave it to him." As Stanton started to leave, Lincoln asked, "What are you going to do with the letter now?" "Mail it, of course," replied Stanton. "Nonsense," Lincoln responded. "You don't want to send that letter. Put it in the stove! That's what I do when I have written a letter while I'm angry. You had a good time writing that letter, now forget about it."

Most of us on a daily basis encounter things that are wrong with other people, our family, our church, our government, our friends, our boss, our employees. . . . The awareness of imperfection is a daily event in our lives. The resolve to live from your values and not live from a "takeover" of what went wrong around you will keep your head and heart going in the right direction.

CHAPTER NINE

THE FORCE OF WORDS

The question is not "Are my words a force?" but rather, "What *kind* of force are my words creating? What happens when I speak?"

- Do people get encouraged or discouraged?
- Is there greater clarity or confusion?
- Do people feel that I care or that I am careless?
- Do I make mountains or move mountains?
- Do I create problems or solve problems?
- Do I create heaviness or do I help people "lighten up"?
- Do I ignite fear or faith?
- Do I tear down or build up?

Words spoken are more than a sound, they are a creative force. Words initiate life or death (Proverbs 18:21), strength or weakness, good or evil. A glance at the past verifies the power of words. Words set in motion and created what we now look back on and refer to as history. The words of people, like Abraham Lincoln and Martin Luther King, Jr., awakened our nation's conscience and pointed us toward the goal of justice and equality. Winston Churchill gave a nation that was discouraged a word picture of courage that inspired them to "Never Give Up." Patrick Henry's words, "Give me liberty or give me death," made a connection with his countrymen and set in motion a victorious fight for freedom. How different would our history be if those timely, well-communicated words would not have been spoken? What if these words of inspiration and faith, that are now a part of history, were replaced with words of discouragement and fear? What battles would not have been won? How different would our lives be today?

The Underestimated Power of Words

The new president of a golf club where I have membership, recently lost the support of some members because of something he said in a monthly newsletter. It was only one line in an otherwise well-written letter, but it caused such a stir that he felt obligated to write a letter of apology for his careless remarks. By the tone of his letter, I could tell how surprised he was that his words had caused such a major reaction from people. The truth is that most people underestimate the power of their words. People, in general, have a difficult time accepting the fact that "mere" words create a response from the world around us. By choosing our words wisely, we have the power to navigate our way past potential crisis and unnecessary hardship. By choosing right words, we can make it through a day filled with potential "land mines" without getting hurt.

One Sunday afternoon, a grandpa laid down on his sofa to take a nap. His grandchildren decided to have a little fun, so they snuck up on him and put limburger cheese on his mustache. When the smell of the cheese woke him up, he asked, "What stinks in this living room?" Going into the kitchen he noticed that the kitchen had the odor too. Muttering to himself, he walked down the hall, through each room in the house, only to find that every room smelled the same. Desperately, he made his way outside for a breath of fresh air. Much to his surprise, the open air brought no relief and he shouted, "The whole world stinks!" A lot of people, like grandpa, don't realize the stink in their life is being created by something right under their nose! When a person underestimates the power of their words, they assume that their problems are originating "out there somewhere" rather than realizing they are right under their own nose shaped and formed by "mere" words.

How Your Words Affect Your Spirit

"Whoever of you loves life and desires to see many good days, keep your tongue from evil..."
— Psalm 34:12-13

By changing your vocabulary, (the words you consistently use) you can change your spirit which will change your life experience. Our own spirit responds to the nature, tone and message of the words we speak. For example, on any given night, millions of parents can be found using the power of words to create a restful night of sleep for their children. The lullabies they sing, the prayers they pray and the words of assurance they speak, send their children into a place of peace and rest. The absence of that parent's voice can create a very different experience for the same child. In much the same way, as adults, our spirits still respond daily to the words we hear. Although we have no control over what others say, our own voice is the voice we hear most. *Just as a parent's voice can change the way a child feels, our own voice can change how we feel.* This will mean the difference between "fight" or "flight" in times of adversity. It will mean the difference between feeling strong or weak. The Bible says, *"Let the weakling say 'I am strong'"* *(2 Corinthians 12:10)*.

In other words, use the force of your words to change your feelings of weakness into feelings of strength. By changing words that create discouragement to words that create encouragement, we change what was going to be an experience of defeat into an experience of victory.

Roger Staubach, former NFL quarterback and Hall of Famer, was once asked how he felt when he had blown a pass. He said, "I can hardly wait to get my hands on the ball again." That internal dialogue is the reason he was a great quarterback. When most would be telling themselves, "You've blown it," champions like Staubach are telling themselves, "Next time will be different."

Verbal Prisons

The prisons we create with our tongue are sometimes created by casual conversations. Statements like, "I hate my hair," or "I hate this house," or "I hate my school," actually heighten the dislike we have and intensify the misery we feel. We all have certain things about ourselves we would change if we could, and for me, one of those is my hair. My hair has a mind of its own. It's straight, flat and untrainable. In one styling salon, they referred to me as the preacher with the hair from hell. For that reason I used to get perms and now I keep my hair short. My hair hasn't changed over the years, but how I deal with it has. Now, I'm just thankful to have hair! At one time I thought I had bad hair, but now I'm realizing that my hair is better than no hair at all! As we go through life, we could all do ourselves a favor by realizing that maturity requires us to change our opinions as we progress in life. We recognize immaturity as an individual whose body has developed with time, but their thinking got "stuck." I see people who form and express opinions before their thinking has matured. They then make another mistake by "pledging allegiance" to the opinion and "aiming" the opinion. Once that opinion sets up – it's in "concrete." This is how people create verbal prisons. They are on a mission to prove to anyone who will listen, that what they have said for years is true. Verbal prisons sound like this:

- "My hair is the absolute worst – nobody can do anything with it."
- "I can't focus on anything for more than thirty seconds."
- "I am the world's worst cook."
- "I don't have time to exercise."
- "I'm burnt out."
- "I'll never be able to forgive them."
- "I don't trust men."

- "I'll never be happy unless…"
- "I'm not a churchgoing kind of person."

On a Sunday after church, a mother came forward with her teenage son and asked that I pray for her husband to have a change of heart towards our church. As I got more of her story, I realized that the husband had professed for years to being a Christian, but he didn't like "big" churches. The son had begun attending our youth ministry, got saved, and his life had been drastically changed. The mom, excited about the positive changes in her son, was now coming to church with him, but the dad was refusing to come. It seemed he had taken a position against larger churches, and even though his son's life had been changed from bad to good, this father was opposed to their attending our church. "All the big churches want is your money," he said. Apparently, standing on his soapbox of opinion meant more to him than supporting what God was doing in his wife and son's life. This is the nature of a verbal prison. It locks people up causing them to close out reasonable and rational thinking. When this happens, people miss out on God's plan for their life. Stop and consider what kind of verbal prisons you may have created for yourself. Are your own words keeping you from experiencing new and better things in your life?

How to Use Words As a Positive Force in Your Life

The Proverbs speak of words as having tremendous potential and influence in our everyday lives.

"Pleasant words are a honeycomb, sweet to the soul and healing to the bones."

— *Proverbs 16:24*

"Through the blessing of the upright a city is exalted."

— *Proverbs 11:11*

"From the fruit of his lips a man enjoys good things."

— *Proverbs 13:2*

"The tongue of the wise brings healing."

—*Proverbs 12:18*

"The tongue has the power of life and death."

— *Proverbs 18:21*

Six Things You Can Do to Use Your Words As a Positive Force

1. **Speak to build others up.** *"Do not let any unwholesome talk come out of your mouths, but only what is helpful for building others up according to their needs, that it may benefit*

those who listen" (Ephesians 4:29). It was on the athletic fields that I first discovered the power of encouraging words. Those single one-liners aimed in my direction by teammates, coaches and friends added unbelievable meaning to a game. They sounded like this, "C'mon, Kevin," "You can do it, Kevin," "Hang in there, Kevin," "You're the man, Kevin," "Shake it off, Kevin," "You'll get 'em next time, Kevin." Although I left the baseball diamonds and the football fields, I've never been able to get away from my yearning to belong to a team where we exchanged encouragement every day. As a result, Sheila, Jodi and I have built this kind of dialogue into our daily vocabulary.

I've made it a part of the culture in our church staff and leadership team. Everyone is worth encouraging and everyone performs better when others encourage them. Although it's common, everyday conversation for some of us, I know that many who read this book live in homes and work in atmospheres where encouragement is a foreign language. If a person has not spoken words of affirmation and blessing to others, it is awkward and uncomfortable at first. However, the more you speak encouraging words, the more comfortable it is. Eventually it will be part of your everyday conversation. People who are "good-finders" sharpen their ability to notice the good in others, which in turn, provides them with opportunities to compliment others. It's also important to note that building others up doesn't necessarily mean lengthy or specific conversation. Simple phrases often work best and are more natural. The Bible says that the Christian life is like running a race. Short, simple phrases can go a long way and never get old. I recommend building these kinds of phrases into your everyday vocabulary. "You're doing great," "Keep it up," "You're awesome," "Way to go," "You made my day," "Fantastic," "Great job," "You're incredible," "You're a genius," "You're the man," "What a gal." Specific and more lengthy encouragement can come at opportune times, but this kind of encouragement can go a long way in building up people in everyday common circumstances.

2. Speak without complaining or arguing. *"Do everything without complaining or arguing…" (Philippians 2:14).*

Complaining – I remember hearing the story of a monk who was only allowed to speak two words every seven years. At the end of his first seven years, his overseer asked him what he would like to say. He said, "Bed hard," and turned and walked back into his silent world. At the end of another seven years in the monastery the overseer asked him what he would like to say. He said, "Food bad," and turned and walked back into his silent world. After another seven years, the overseer again asked him what he would like to say. He said, "I quit." "It's a good thing," said the overseer, "All you do is complain!" As funny as this sounds, it's not how often you make a complaint, but rather how much of your conversation is complaining in nature. Complaining can creep into a person's vocabulary undetected and unnoticed by the person themselves. These people don't recognize their complaining, because they can't remember the last time they made a "formal complaint." However, their conversation is filled with expressions and innuendoes that are complaint oriented. Almost every time they speak they refer to something they are unhappy about. Don't let complaining creep into your conversation.

Arguing – As I write this chapter, we are building the Champions Centre, a forty thousand square foot youth and children's facility. The new facility is connected to our church dome by an atrium. The atrium is designed as a spacious "mall-like" area with bookstores, coffee shops, information centers and social settings. Sheila and I are coffee drinkers, so we approached a coffee company about putting in a store in the atrium. After several meetings, we had met all of the company's criteria for a store and it appeared to be a done deal. On the verge of finalizing everything, someone within their company decided they did not want to be that closely connected to a faith-based organization. They were willing to put in a smaller kiosk sales counter but did not want to put in a full-blown store. As I listened to the explanation they gave me, I could not understand any of the logic and reason behind their decision. Several times in our conversations, the disagreement almost escalated into arguments. I felt they were being unreasonable and unfair, but I finally had to accept their decision or turn the disagreement into an argument. *I always try to remember that when disagreements are being discussed, if it escalates into an argument – nobody wins.* Since then, another coffee company was approached and they agreed to put in a store at our site. The first company has since decided that their position was wrong, so they have apologized and asked to be reconsidered as a store on our site. We're considering our best option. Arguments can close the door on future relationships. Arguments create verbal prisons that are hard to get out of. Disagreements can provide a healthy exchange of thoughts, ideas and perspective. Arguments, however, benefit no one and usually do irreparable harm.

3. Don't talk too much. *"The more the words, the less the meaning and how does that profit anyone?" (Ecclesiastics 6:11).*

Excessive talking wearies others – when you're in a conversation, make sure you don't ignore the body language of the person you are talking to. It may not be a good time for them to listen to the testimony or story you want to share. When I travel to speak, I can always tell when the driver has been trained to not talk too much. Sometimes I will initiate more talk by asking questions. Other times, I appreciate not feeling like I have to talk and being able to focus on my message or relax.

Excessive talking will distract you from your responsibilities – Some of the greatest socializers in the world struggle financially, because they get distracted and lead unproductive lives. Talking on the phone too much will cause the laundry to pile up, the dishes to stay dirty and the bed to not be made.

Excessive talking can cheapen your words – Remember the price goes up when there's a shortage! People who talk a lot have less chance of being listened to than those who speak sparingly. Sometimes when a person rambles, they will say some good things, but nobody hears what they would have heard in an edited version.

Excessive talking will lead to sin – When I was a teenager, a magnet on my mother's refrigerator said,

"It's better to remain silent and thought a fool, then to speak up and remove all doubt." The Proverbs says, *"Where words are many sin is not absent" (Proverbs 10:19).* The more you talk, the higher the possibility that you will say something you will regret later. Lies, criticisms, gossip, and stupidity spill out of mouths that are open too much.

4. **Speak without gossiping.** *"A gossip betrays confidence..." "A gossip separates close friends..." "Without gossip a quarrel dies down..." (Proverbs 11:13; 16:28; 26:20).*
It has been said that there is so much bad in the best of us, and so much that is good in the worst of us; that it doesn't behoove any of us to talk about the rest of us. Gossip is not always as accurate as it's made out to be. Once it has traveled through the "grapevine" it becomes a distortion of information. Gossips are the small people in life. They usually have poor self-esteem and have such little going on in their own life that they have time to talk about other people. Gossip almost always originates in a person who is bitter or has an ax to grind. We've become somewhat accustomed to having people gossiping about us. A couple of years ago, an ugly rumor about Sheila and I created a follow-up by members of our staff who wanted to get to the source of the rumor. It all hit the fan one day when

a former staff member called a current staff member to let them know that they had heard about the investigation into my private life. They proceeded to offer "comfort" to the staff member saying that they were praying for them. When our staff member said, "What are you talking about?" the person said, "Oh maybe you haven't yet heard...Pastors Kevin and Sheila are going to be indited on charges of misappropriating funds and money laundering." With such an unfounded and bizarre rumor floating around, my staff investigated and traced it back to a former, disgruntled staff member and a former attendee of our church who was starting his own church a few blocks away from ours. When you're tempted to gossip, read the seven things God hates in Proverbs 6:16-19. Then go look in the mirror and remind yourself it's time for you to "get a life."

5. **Speak without criticizing others.** Sometimes people who are trying to avoid being a critic must discuss an unpleasant situation in another person's life, with a mutual friend or associate. For example, a director on our staff may need to discuss with me a situation involving someone working in their department who is unproductive, has a bad attitude, or is difficult to work with. Those kinds of discussions by people who hold others accountable are very different in

nature than the criticism spoken daily about people in higher positions at work, church, and government. It's also very different in nature than the criticism that goes on in a home by a wife about her husband, or a father about his children. I've always wanted to put the following words of Theodore Roosevelt in one of my books and this is the right place for it. Even if you've read it before, read it again. *"It is not the critic who counts, not the person who points out where the doer of deeds could have done better. The credit belongs to the person who is actually in the arena; whose face is marred by dust and sweat and blood; who strives valiantly; who errs and comes up short again and again; who knows the great enthusiasms, the devotions, and spends himself or herself in a worthy cause; who at best knows in the end the triumph of high achievement; and at worst, at least fails while daring greatly; so that his or her place shall never be with those cold and timid souls who know neither victory nor defeat."*

It's not the critic who counts. . . . Critics sit in the grandstands with a lot to say but nothing beneficial. What is said in the grandstands doesn't put points on the board and doesn't win a game. When you find yourself limited to a grandstand position, unable to get down on the field, at least make sure you choose cheerleading over criticizing.

6. Speak at the highest level of your faith. *"It is written: 'I believed; therefore I have spoken.' With that same spirit of faith we also believe and therefore speak"* (*2 Corinthians 4:13*).

Everyone has thoughts of defeat. Discouraging thoughts enter into everyone's mind. Doubts and fears gain access more often than most of us like to admit. The same mind, however, produces hope, dreams, and faith-oriented thoughts. The same mind that causes someone to think, "What if (something bad) happens?" also thinks, "What if (something good) happens?" In the above Scripture, the writer, Apostle Paul, is making the point that his own mentors spoke in alignment with their faith and that he too, was choosing to speak according to his *beliefs* not his doubts, worries or fears. That doesn't mean he didn't have doubts, worries or fears. It just means he was choosing what to verbally acknowledge and talk about. A thought increases in power when it's spoken. Faith comes by hearing (Romans 10:17) and so does fear. Whatever you speak increases in your life. You can speak self-defeating proclamations like, "I'll never get out of this mess," or "I can't stand all this stress." On the other hand, you can choose to give your faith a voice. Even when the negative thoughts are louder, you can still choose to locate those quieter voices of faith and speak believable words of confidence and hope. When you do, you will immediately feel the positive force you've created by speaking at the highest level of your faith. Imagine that in your mind you have a lion of fear and a lion of faith. Imagine that your words are lion food. When you speak your faith, you feed the faith lion within you and neglect the fear lion. The more you do this, the stronger the faith lion grows and the weaker the fear lion becomes. Speaking according to your faith will feed your faith and starve your fears. As the lion of faith grows within you, your words of faith take on a forceful role, setting your course and shaping your future.

CONCLUSION

This book is about taking responsibility for your life and future. In our world a lot of people claim to be victims and others learn helplessness as if it were an art. But God, in His great love, has offered each of us the "opportunity of a lifetime." I hope this book encourages you, as a reader, to "seize the opportunity."

It's All Up to You

- Your successes depend upon you.
- Your happiness depend on you.
- You have to steer your own course.
- You have to shape your own future.
- You have to educate yourself.
- You have to do your own thinking.
- You have to live with your own conscience.
- Your mind is yours and can be used only by you.
- You come into this world alone.
- You go to the grave alone.
- You are alone with your inner thoughts during the journey between.
- You must make your own decisions.
- You must abide by the consequences of your acts.
- You alone can regulate your habits and make or unmake your health.
- You alone can assimilate things mental and things material.

- You have to do your own assimilation all through life.
- You may be taught by a teacher, but you have to absorb the knowledge. She cannot transfuse it into your brain.
- You alone can control your mind cells and your brain cells.
- You may have spread before you the wisdom of the ages, but unless you assimilate it you derive no benefit from it; no one can force it into your cranium.
- You alone can control your own muscles.
- You must stand on your own feet, physically and metaphorically.
- You must take your own steps.
- You must take control of your mental and physical machinery, and make something of yourself.
- You cannot have battles fought for you. You must fight them yourself.
- You have to be the captain of your own destiny.
- You have to master your own faculties.
- You have to solve your own problems.
- You have to form your own ideals.
- You have to create your own ideas.
- You must govern your own tongue.
- Your real life is your own thoughts.
- Your thoughts are of your own making.
- Your character is your own handiwork.
- You alone can select the materials that go into it.
- You alone can reject what is not fit to go into it.
- You are the creator of your own personality.
- You can be disgraced by no person's hand but your own.

- You have to write your own record.
- You have to build your own monument – or dig your own pit.

Which are you doing?

(Alexander Lockhart, Author)

Other Books by this Author:

Characteristics of a Winner

Developing Confidence

Raising Champion Children

The Proving Ground

Pardon Me, I'm Prospering

Author Contact Information

**Kevin Gerald Communications
c/o Champions Centre, home of
Covenant Celebration Church
1819 E. 72nd Street
Tacoma, WA 98404**

www.kevingerald.com

NOTES

NOTES